COMPLICATED

LIVES

COMPLICATED

LIVES

Sophisticated Consumers,
Intricate Lifestyles,
Simple Solutions

Michael
Willmott
and
William
Nelson

WILEY

Other Wiley Editorial Offices
John Wiley & Sons Inc.,
111 River Street, Hoboken, NJ 07030, USA

Jossey-Bass,
989 Market Street, San Francisco, CA 94103–1741, USA

Wiley-VCH Verlag GmbH,
Boschstr. 12, D-69469 Weinheim, Germany

John Wiley & Sons Australia Ltd,
33 Park Road, Milton, Queensland 4064, Australia

John Wiley & Sons (Asia) Pte Ltd,
2 Clementi Loop #02–01, Jin Xing Distripark, Singapore 129809

John Wiley & Sons Canada Ltd,
22 Worcester Road, Etobicoke, Ontario, Canada M9W 1L1

Wiley also publishes its books in a variety of electronic formats. Some content that appears in print may not be available in electronic books.

Library of Congress Cataloging-in-Publication Data
Willmott, Michael, 1952–
    Complicated lives: sophisticated consumers, intricate lifestyles, simple solutions/Michael Willmott and William Nelson.
        p. cm.
    Includes bibliographical references and index.
    ISBN 0–470–85701–3 (cloth)
    1. Consumption (Economics)   2. Economic history–1945–
    3. Social history–1945–   I. Nelson, William, 1974–   II. Title.
    HC79.C6.W55 2003
    339.4′7–dc21   2003012573

British Library Cataloguing in Publication Data
A catalogue record for this book is available from the British Library

ISBN 0-470-85701-3

Typeset in 11.5/15 Bembo by Florence Production Ltd, Stoodleigh, Devon
Printed and bound in Great Britain by TJ International, Padstow, Cornwall

This book is printed on acid-free paper responsibly manufactured from sustainable forestry, in which at least two trees are planted for each one used for paper production.

CONTENTS

INTRODUCTION

LIFE COULD BE EASIER

Although we hope you lead a fulfilling and, in your own terms, successful existence, does it not sometimes just feel all too busy, too stressful? Does there not seem to be so much to do and so little time to do it?

This is the cliché of modern life. It doesn't matter whether you are a high-flying business person, a concerned media commentator, a dedicated public service worker, a retired executive with a hectic social life or a parent with a full-time commitment to your family – your life is likely to feel busy.

Why is this? A number of explanations have been put forward. Some argue that capitalism and its promotion of materialism inevitably leads to a hurly-burly jostling for position as people compete to differentiate themselves by buying more and more material goods[1]. In this argument, it is, effectively, all the fault of consumer culture – we are encouraged to buy much more than we either really need or want. Others blame technology. The continual roll-out of new technologies fuels, and frustrates, materialistic desire but also, literally, quickens the pace of life[2]. Rapid innovation creates a sense of a world changing at an ever-faster rate; while some of the technologies themselves enable things to be done more quickly[3]. Microwave ovens allow meal preparation to be reduced to seconds, while mobile phones enable people to be in contact at all times. Other commentators have claimed that globalization and the increasing power of multinational companies is making work both less secure and more demanding[4]. Related to this, some suggest that changing work practices and the increasing involvement of women in the workforce mean that work takes an increasing chunk of people's waking hours, leading to 'overwork' and less time for leisure[5].

To these doom-laden prognoses can be added the theories of people like Robert Putnam[6] and Richard Sennett[7] who worry about the erosion of the communities and work environments that we used to inhabit. Such writers seem to yearn for some bygone era when everyone knew their place and had a happier and less harassed existence. A related strain consists of those who argue that we lead atomized, impersonal lives, locked away in a couch potato existence as we spend more and more time watching television or on the Internet, consuming 'virtual' (and insufficiently 'real') experiences[8].

Often, these arguments are used to support the thesis that the world is somehow worse nowadays – and, indeed, that we need to turn back the clock to a time when the world was more relaxed, cohesive and, it is argued, happier. (Although how this might be proved is highly unclear – for what it's worth, questions asking people how happy they are have shown little change over 50 years[9].)

Aside from the considerable practical difficulties of reversing change in such a way, we suspect that few citizens would welcome the reality of the world as it used to be. People may have rose-tinted memories of the past but actually living there was a somewhat more challenging experience than their romanticized view would suggest.

And the negative take on life today hardly fits the facts. As we show in this book, work time over the course of the average year has not increased significantly (indeed for some it has decreased) and where it has, as for women, it is generally the result of a deliberate choice. Contrary to popular belief, community and social life is amazingly resilient. Sure, it has changed, but humans are social beings who on the whole actively seek, and enjoy, opportunities to meet, mix and converse. That is why some technologies, and particularly communication ones, have been so successful – people just love to talk. Other technologies are also enriching people's lives, either by relieving them from the chores of daily living (hand washing clothes or dishes, for example) or by enhancing experiences of learning, entertainment and communication. Of course, many new products are technology-led rather than consumer-led with unwelcome consequences, as we point out in Chapter 6, but technology per se is not making the world a worse place[10]. And all our research suggests that not only do many people love shopping – particularly that which involves discretionary items – but that competitive differentiation is not the bane of most people's lives.

So why, then, do things seem so hectic? We have a simple answer: it is because life has become so complicated.

This is the paradox of progress. Today's generation is richer, healthier, safer and enjoys more freedom than any in the past. Yet life seems more pressured because it is more complex. The discretion and choice that the modern era offers also require decisions. And, increasingly, these are those most difficult of decisions – those with multiple options.

This is the critical issue of life today – how to benefit from the positive developments without being drowned in the complexities that ensue. How, in this world, do we avoid feeling overwhelmed by it all? Is this the reason why self-reported levels of stress and anxiety (albeit a notoriously inaccurate measure of health) are increasing across the western world? These issues and this conundrum are what this book is about.

There is, however, an important caveat to our thesis – and this is that it does not apply to all members of societies, or not in the way we discuss it in this book. Our focus here is on the affluent majority – perhaps 70% of the population. It is they who are afflicted with the complaint of complexity. For the less fortunate, life is difficult but for different reasons to those outlined in our first chapter. They simply struggle with the ordeals of first making ends meet and then trying to become part of the affluent and complex society that many of them aspire to belong to.

This leads to an interesting and provocative suggestion: that the two main issues facing society today are deprivation (and, increasingly, polarization and detachment) and complication. Here, then, we have the real challenge facing not only governments but business too: how to cater for the increasing demands of the affluent majority, while addressing the needs of the deprived minority. For businesses this implies understanding not only the complexity of modern consumer (and employee) life but also their broader roles and relationships with society as a whole[11].

We believe the idea of 'complicated lives' is a useful metaphor for assessing what's right and what's wrong in the modern world and for identifying the solutions to people's problems. If we can understand why people have unnecessary and unsubstantiated fears and why – despite more free time and more discretion and longer, healthier lives – they feel more pressured, we can start to develop remedies.

The root cause of the phenomenon we describe is that we want, and expect, more from life. Understanding this simple fact – that people have higher expectations, more varied choices and more complex decisions – is critically important. We believe managing complexity, or helping people to manage it, will be one of the most crucial issues of the 21st century.

Although this book is primarily aimed at business readers it should also be of use to public sector managers. But we hope that people also find it interesting and useful from a personal perspective

– in helping them understand and respond to the complexity of their own lives. Perhaps by understanding life's complications, we can all reap the benefits that the affluence, health and freedom of the modern world potentially provide.

CHAPTER 1

IT'S A COMPLICATED LIFE

*G*o into a hypermarket anywhere across the world and think what it would feel like for someone transported from the 1950s into the present day. The range of goods would seem incredible: exotic fruits, Asian spices; wines from around the world, compact discs, light bulbs and home appliances like microwave ovens or even televisions. There would be a fantastic, and to our 1950s visitor an unbelievable, array of brands, sub-brands and varieties. There would not be just Coke or Pepsi but diet, caffeine-free, cherry and now vanilla versions of cola too. Then there would be the own-brands. The choice would seem huge, unimaginable and unmanageable.

Even those of us brought up in the modern era sometimes find the choice simply overwhelming. In a personal example, one of us was looking for orange juice in a grocery store in Florida. Of course there was the issue of brand choice, but the real complication came with the different varieties – eight in all for the world's leading fruit juice brand, Tropicana. Some had added calcium, others were 'low acid'; there was one specially for children and another with double vitamins. The process of deciding what was wanted did not take long – but finding it took several minutes.

The same is true across the world. Thus shops supply many different types of dental floss (14 in one British pharmacy we visited) or brandy (too numerous to count in a Spanish hypermarket) or microwave ovens (22 models in a French hypermarket). And this range of choices permeates throughout our lives. Homes hold a far greater inventory of foods, drinks and personal care products (to match the individual household members' tastes, or health concerns) and of cleaning and washing products (to match different tasks). Our music choices are more varied with a typical home having many more CDs than our parents would have had LPs and cassettes. There is a much wider range of beers, wines and spirits to be found in bars. And we have more TVs in our homes (with around a hundred times more channels to choose from than twenty years ago) so that different members of the household can watch what they want, not to mention the increased options arising from video tapes, DVDs and video-on-demand. This is just one example of how our lives are more complicated than they were for our friend from the 1950s. But a large number of developments are adding to the complexity of life.

This book is about such complexity and the challenges and opportunities that it presents to companies and other organizations seeking to be consumer-led. We believe that not only is this a fundamentally new way of considering consumer attitudes and behaviour but it provides the tools for successfully delivering the solutions that consumers need. Our basic thesis is that life is better but it is more complex. Understand that and you start to really understand what consumers want and need; what will help their lives and what will not; what will be successful and what will fail.

In this book we show why life is becoming more complex and the stresses and strains it places on people. We show why companies have to provide more choice but also need to have strong and trusted brands. We discuss the types of advice that consumers will welcome and how technological innovation can help but also exacerbate people's problems. We explain why employment policies will have to become more flexible and consumer response mechanisms more alert.

Aware that our readers will suffer from the very same complexity that we are writing about, we have written this first chapter in the form of an executive summary. In it we review all the main arguments and some of the conclusions. Read in conjunction with the final chapter on the implications for business it provides a 'fast track' overview of our thesis. The other chapters deal in detail with the different components that make up our complicated lives.

WHY IS LIFE BECOMING MORE COMPLEX?

When we say life is more complicated, what do we mean? What are the processes that are driving this change and why do we accept it?

We have already hinted at one of the reasons – the range of choices available to consumers, even in the more mundane aspects of their daily living. This very much reflects the empowering capabilities of rising affluence that allows people to indulge in, and embrace, a wider range of wishes. This is the paradox of economic growth; it is an enabler but it is also a complicator.

But it is not just a question of affluence – economic growth sustains a wide range of factors that are making life more complicated (Figure 1.1).

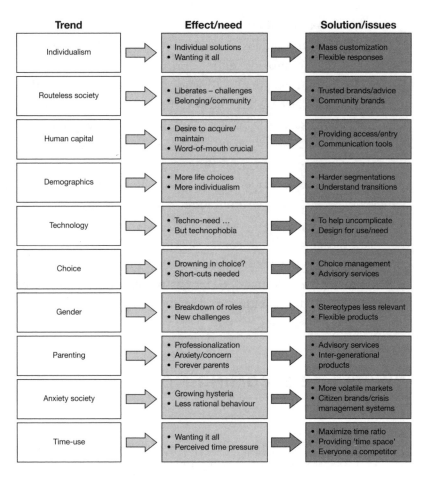

Figure 1.1   The factors making life more complicated.

Source: Future Foundation.

The rise of the new individualism

First is the rise of what we might call the new individualism. Of course, economics again is an issue here. Most people, being more financially empowered, can exercise greater discretion with their purchases and, even more fundamentally, have less to lose when they buy the wrong thing – making a mistake is less painful. We buy clothes we never wear, food we do not eat and books we have no time to read[1]. Many commentators have noted[2] that there is something about the development of human society that encourages the definition of the self to be more individualized – put bluntly, people are happier doing their own thing. This economic discretion and the growth of individualism mean that consumers require, indeed insist upon, more choice. Not only do we have the means and desire to do our own thing but we also want to do much *more*; we want to 'have it all'. As individual players in a world where barriers to what you can and cannot do have largely broken down, we expect to be able to be good parents, have a great career and lead fulfilling and exciting lives outside the worlds of family and work. But wanting it all and, more stressfully, expecting it all obviously have consequences.

Key issues

- Individualism means people want individual solutions. We foresee the market further splitting between the hand-made premium end providing authentic and unique offers and the mass customized end, providing an element of difference but at a price people can afford. Mass customization can take the form of built to order[3] (as in Dell Computers' business model) or through increasing sub-branding and varietization (as with Tropicana). To some extent, of course, this will depend on the market in question.
- Young inexperienced consumers can be daunted by choice. With their lower confidence in their position and identity in society they have more need of brands. But with such consumers, and older ones too, brands will be appropriated to mean different things to different people. Brands

will have a choice between being chameleons – allowing people to take their own meanings from them – or being audacious – boldly stating their position and asking people to 'take us or leave us'. In a sense, this is the branding analogue of the two forms of mass customization mentioned above.

■ Wanting it all creates time pressures (see below) and requires flexible responses from service providers.

The routeless society – the decline in deference

Alongside, and interplaying with, the new individualism is the declining influence of a range of established institutions. Again, populist views about this are not entirely correct. These talk about the decline in trust in institutions and while there is some evidence of this it is not universally true. For example, in a MORI poll in Britain, the proportion of the general public saying (in 2003) that they trust the police, government ministers and TV news readers to tell the truth has not changed much since 1983. Indeed, the proportions trusting doctors and teachers have risen. A way to describe our relationships with such institutions and such professions is that we show less deference towards them – their views have less impact on our own life choices. There are fewer 'givens' in life. In the past, people's moral, ethical or social decisions were more likely to be determined by others: the church, the government, elders in the family or the class you came from. Now this is less true. For many people this is a liberating experience (although it is not seen like this for some of those on the right of the political spectrum) but it can bring problems. With fewer 'givens', people have less guidance and fewer 'signposts'. They have to plot their own life strategies; make their own choices. With fewer set courses, life becomes more complicated. As it becomes more complex and as the deference towards traditional institutions wanes, so there is a growing interest (contrary to the claims of many critics) in various guises of community.

Key issues

- People will increasingly seek and welcome help and guidance. The key question is how far companies can offer this and how much it will come from other agencies. Financial advice is an obvious area but other life planning services might prosper too. The role of brands will be important – trusted brands that can solve problems or even run parts of people's lives. (But note, the cost of failure – when so much has been invested in a brand/company – will be that much greater too.) We refer to the role of brands and consumer choices elsewhere; here we are talking about brands and life choices.

- The decline in deference to traditional institutions is encouraging a need and demand for new community attachments. Some of these are local (note the growth in local and regional identity across the world) and some are built around activities (communities of interest). So there will be good opportunities for brands with strong community/local ties who take 'citizenship' seriously. Opportunities will arise for special interest clubs like Kimberly-Clark's *Huggies Club* in the UK that builds on the company's nappy (diaper) brand to provide an information and advice forum for young parents.

- In a more 'routeless' world, heritage (and heritage brands) are likely to have an additional leverage they can draw on.

Human capital and the network society

As the traditional constraints and controls of institutions, classes, religions, communities and families have waned, so the need to manage connections and networks has become more important. Sociologist Manuel Castells describes the defining zeitgeist of the times as the 'network society'[4] – the critical thing nowadays is who you know and who you are connected to; the communities (in the broadest sense) that you are part of or have access to. Jeremy Rifkin, an economist, believes access to networks is becoming more and more important[5]. Work by social scientists at Essex University in Britain also suggests that such networks are of rising significance (see Chapter 3). Again, the outcome here does not chime with popular belief. To take families as one example, it is clear that the potential influence of parents is growing. Although their ability to proscribe what their children might or should do is decreasing, their role in providing access to services and networks is becoming more crucial. The same is true of other institutions – their strength and importance to the individual comes not from pre-determining life courses and individual actions but from providing options and life chances through their access to networks of suitably minded people, services and organizations. The importance of networks is, of course, heightened by the new technologies that we consider later. But, and this is the critical point, the very essence of negotiating and managing networks is not only constantly evolving but is, in itself, complicated, requiring a range of social and other skills.

Related to the increasing importance of networks and the skills required to navigate them – what we refer to as 'social capital' – is the growth in what has been called 'cultural capital'. In a service economy, it is access to services, networks and the *consumption of culture* that is important, argues Rifkin in his book, *Age of Access*. Echoing the work of influential French sociologist Pierre Bourdieu, Rifkin maintains that the critical currency of the modern world is cultural capital. This is the knowledge and experience of arts, culture and hobbies that help to define who we are and, critically, differentiate us from others (can you talk authoritatively about opera, wine or even Big Brother?). Rifkin argues we are moving from an era of industrial to cultural capitalism where 'cultural production is increasingly becoming the dominant form of economic activity' and 'securing access to the many cultural resources and experiences that nurture one's psychological existence becomes just as important as holding property'. Whether the culture is 'high' (opera?) or 'low' (celebrity watching?), you can differentiate yourself, gain kudos and access to opportunities by having cultural knowledge or experience ('been to the match', 'seen the play'); by having cultural capital. This is important because surely the management of this 'cultural' capital is more complex than that of physical goods. As Rifkin points out, 'They are immaterial and intangible. They are performed not produced. They exist only at the moment they are rendered. They cannot be held, accumulated, or inherited.' In other words they (the components of cultural capital) need to be maintained and nurtured on a regular basis. This is another pressure in modern life that we believe is critically important in understanding the complications people face.

Key issues

- The market for experiences generally will continue to grow as people seek to build cultural capital. So, too, will the interest in putting some form of experience into more mundane activities (like some forms of shopping).
- But, the implicit barriers to entry for cultural activities (defined in the broad sense we are using here) mean that consumers will be open to ways of gaining 'easy entry'.

This could be advisory services but could be built on brands themselves. Australian wine company Penfolds has three main brands, each with its own 'ladder' that one can progress up towards true connoisseurship.

■ Maintaining social networks requires skills in communication and networking. Not only will this promote communication technologies themselves but it will provide opportunities for help and guidance products. Virtual communities on the Internet play a crucial role here.

■ Word-of-mouth will become more important in the network society. Companies need to think about how it can be managed and influenced. Identifying key people, places and attitudes will be important. So too will giving people a (positive) reason to talk about you.

New life courses; new challenges

Together with the economic, social and political changes already outlined are some purely demographic ones that are changing the nature of people's life courses and hence their life choices. People are living longer, retiring earlier, delaying getting married or cohabiting, having children later (and fewer of them) and having a more pronounced period of Bridget Jones style 'singledom' (something that hardly existed at all in the past – people may have been single but they most likely would have lived in the parental home whatever their age). The old progression of living at home, getting married and leaving home, having kids, children leaving home and then retiring has been replaced by a more differentiated and complex set of life-stages. Increasing numbers of people temporarily return home at some point after leaving home, co-habitation, deciding to not have children, divorce and separation, empty-nesting, delayed retirement – all increase the variety of possible stages in life that people can go through.

Perhaps surprisingly, the ageing of the population might be helping to promote this individualism. The more varied and less predictable life courses mean there is, at any given age, a less certain or specific type of arrangement to be expected. Your age no longer determines (or certainly not to the extent that it did in the past) your outlook, attitudes or behaviours in life. And, as we will discuss in Chapter 3, it is arguable that from a neurological point of view an ageing population is likely to be a more individualistic one too.

Key issues

■ An ageing population is not a more boring and settled one. Indeed, it is a more individualistic, dynamic and changing one in which there is less of a set order to things.

■ As life courses become more complex so segmentation will become more complicated, requiring more sophisticated approaches.

■ One way to address this is to monitor and target people by the *transitions* they make in life. This is the new way forward – an alternative to segmentation. Considering the triggers to certain consumer behaviour – the purchase of life insurance or savings instruments, a new oven or a house move – provides a much richer and more accurate way of anticipating consumer interest.

Technology and complexity

So, economic growth and rising affluence, the individualization of society, the declining influence of, and deference to, the prescriptive function of traditional institutions, fewer given roles and lifestyles, the increasing importance of networks and just plain old demographic change all mean life is more complicated but there is another factor that is important too – technology.

Here again is a major paradox of the modern world since in many ways technology is a solver of problems and hence simplifies things; but in reality it often does the opposite. The reason for this is that in periods of rapid technological change, as we are experiencing now, the very pace of change is confusing and disorientating. As Marshall McCluhan once noted[6], 'Innumerable confusions and a feeling of despair invariably emerge in periods of great technological and cultural transition.'

The very nature of some of the new technologies helps to fuel the perception of a faster pace of change. Always on, mobile devices now allow people to be contacted not only at all times but in all places too. Add in the sheer variety of channels that now exists – TVs, phones, personal digital assistants (PDAs), computers – and there is a very real danger of channel overload particularly as it continues to grow with increasing digitalization and bandwidth. Unsurprisingly, orchestrating and controlling this cornucopia of channels (and the interactions between them – you might buy over the Internet, return to a shop and complain via a phone) is a daunting task. The fact that marketers, cold-selling in a number of ingenious ways (such as with those numerous pop-up windows that obscure your chosen web page and are deliberately difficult to close), abuse some of these channels only makes matters worse.

This is not to say that the new communications technologies are not welcome – their tremendous success is testament to the enthusiasm with which they are greeted. They are needed for networking, are valued for their convenience and appreciated for their contribution to that activity that humans love – socializing.

There is also the not insignificant fact that those driving technological innovation and dissemination seem almost to go out of their way to confuse people by overcomplicating the functions and workings of the technology. In their quest to add every techno bell and whistle to their latest wunder-invention they not only provide capabilities that, although the technology can provide it, no one actually wants, but also do so in ways that completely flummox the users whose lives it is meant to improve. For example, over 50% of British consumers do not feel confident in using all the features available on their video recorder. Technology can improve and de-complicate people's lives – think of washing machines, microwaves and personal organizers – but is invariably implemented in such a way as to add to life's complications. Such, as we say, is the paradox of modern life.

Key issues

- The Internet and other communication devices will continue to thrive but success will be most notable for solutions that simplify or offer control/management.
- Don't misuse the new media. The success of many of the new technologies arises from the fact that they are proletarian: social media for sociable people to use.
- A revolution is needed in technology design (and this applies to all products and services, not just digital technology). Designers need to throw off the shackles of techno-determinism (building what is clever or possible) and turn themselves to being user-led/needs-driven (building what people want and need).
- And as part of this don't overload products with features; design for ease of use.

THE MANIFESTATION OF INCREASING COMPLEXITY

So, for a variety of social, political, economic and technological reasons society has changed, and is continuing to change, significantly. There seems little point in moaning about this, or indeed trying to slow or even reverse this development – economic growth is a liberating force that feeds the increasing individualization, choices and complications of modern life. In our view, despite the obvious attractions to some of a back-to-basics agenda it is futile to try to impose more simplistic and rigid lifestyles onto the population. Life is getting more complicated because individuals readily seek those life options that make it more so. We cannot change that basic desire, that basic driver of change, by, for example, telling women that they should not do paid work when they have young children or making divorce more difficult or trying to increase the power of institutions in dictating people's lives. All we can do is try to ameliorate the unintended, and not so nice, consequences of our and others' increased life choices. To understand what we might do, let us consider some of the ways in which life's complications are manifested.

Drowning in choice?

The first, and most obvious, area of complication in our lives is that of overwhelming choice in terms of the products and services we can buy. Some people may wonder whether you really can have too much choice, and certainly in our experience the world seems to divide into those people who immediately relate to the idea and those who do not[7]. What is not in doubt is that nowadays there is a degree of choice unimaginable to our grandparents.

More choice is the result of both demand and supply. Increasing individualism, as we have already pointed out, requires a wider range (or more variations) of consumer goods and services. We expect, and can afford to pay for, things that satisfy our own personal needs. Wherever you look in modern life there is more choice; and on the whole that is because there is a demand for it.

On the supply side, globalization has opened up markets and broadened tastes. Partly through access to global media, partly through travel and partly through supply push into new markets, people are exposed to, and embrace, a wider range of cultures and the different tastes and product formulation that implies. As trade barriers reduce, international players can enter more markets, bringing with them their own ideas on what local consumers might like (not always successfully it has to be said). This broadens choice but also increases competition for national players which, in itself, is a spur to innovation and new product design by local producers.

So consumers, at an aggregate level, want more choice and producers are − on the whole − able to offer it (indeed, some have suggested that companies may increase the number of varieties deliberately to confuse consumers). Yet this provokes complication for two reasons. First, although at a market level there may be a demand for greater choice (and a growing one as tastes fragment), at an individual level there may not be: some people are just not interested in some markets. For any given product or service − cars, hi-fi, holidays or life insurance − there will be people who want more choice and those who want less. The result is that for many consumers in many markets an excess of choice is, indeed, a burden. Second, even where people might want choice, they do not have the mechanisms and information to negotiate the available options.

Consumers have to develop strategies to deal with the explosion of choice. These range from seeking the advice of friends or professionals, to using price as a filtering process, to relying on brands as their choice managers. We discuss these strategies and the implications for organizations more fully in a later chapter. Here we will restrict ourselves to making the point that an understanding of this process is critical to business success since it helps to illuminate the decision-making mechanisms at work in consumption. This is particularly relevant in low interest markets – which increasingly do not equate with low price markets – where consumers' choices may not be as logical as might be presumed. This is important in developing successful marketing strategies. There is a huge commercial opportunity in providing guides and services that help consumers to navigate the complexities of choice.

Key issues

- With so much choice, consumers need help. There are a number of strategies consumers use but three stand out: using brands as choice managers; seeking advice from others; and price.
- Naomi Klein is wrong when she postulates that people are beginning to reject brands, for one simple reason: branding is a shortcut in the choice-making process. Sony ever let you down with an electronic appliance? Nokia with a mobile phone? Nike with a sports shoe? No – why not start your search with that brand then[8]? This eases the decision-making process when faced with multiple choices, particularly for inexperienced or unconfident consumers. And who can be confident in every market?
- An alternative for consumers is to seek advice. This can be from formal advisers (as in financial services), magazines (who increasingly publish comparative tests), retailers (who hold a tremendous amount of power here but need to ensure their staff are properly trained) and word-of-mouth from friends, family, work colleagues or others (increasingly via the Internet).

- In some markets, particularly low interest ones, people may simply use price as a choice mechanism going for the cheapest, or some combination of brand name and price. In some higher interest, connoisseur markets, those with the financial means may start at the other end (the most expensive). In case anyone doubted it, pricing will remain a hugely important part of the marketing mix despite rising affluence and growing discretionary spending.

Regendering life

Beyond consumption, there are broader challenges to individuals in our increasingly 'routeless' world. No better example exists of the changes created by the collapse of set roles and life courses than that of gender. Over the course of less than two generations the relative role of women (especially) and men has altered beyond recognition. Look at sociological studies from the 1950s[9] or contemporary accounts of life during that period[10] and it is clear how the lives of women (and therefore men) were different. Now, although full equality has not yet been achieved, women have a far greater range of work, family and leisure options. But making these decisions and balancing the conflicts that can arise (for example between work and motherhood) inevitably has its costs. And as more women work so they have more financial control over their lives – another liberation of sorts but an added set of skills that are required. Women, on the whole, find such choices rewarding but they clearly add to the stresses and strains – and the complications – of life. The same is true for men, albeit to a lesser degree. As women's roles have changed so men have needed to adapt too. Again this need not be seen as a negative development since most men welcome the opportunity to, for example, be more involved in their children's upbringing (our research unsurprisingly shows that few men relish taking on the more mundane household chores). But the net result is that for both men and women, roles and responsibilities have become less defined. Life, in this sense, is more complicated.

Key issues

■ Gender stereotypes will become increasingly irrelevant as the differences between men and women continue to erode. Advertising based on gender will have less resonance than in the past.

■ But the new roles each sex is taking on will present opportunities for advice/training/self-help programmes for certain activities.

■ More women have financial discretion and control so will welcome products, services and advice in this area. At the same time there will be opportunities for more flexible financial products for couples that combine mutual liability and individual freedom.

The parenting challenge

It is not only that roles are changing and becoming more open but also that people, as we have suggested, are expecting more from life and thus putting themselves under more pressure to perform. Nowhere is this more obvious than in attitudes towards parenting where the combined pressures of society and individual desire have arguably made the task more demanding than ever. Today's parents are taking child-care more seriously, having more 'quality' time with their kids, engaging with them, while at the same time worrying more. This trend has gone so far that some commentators feel that parents are verging on the paranoid and being over-protective of the children to the detriment of their long-term development and independence[11]. Whether or not this is true, the reality is that parenting appears more complex than it has ever been.

As the family becomes more democratic, with not only more equality between parents (as just noted) but also more voice and notice given to children too, so all decisions become – potentially – more consensual. There is a new level of negotiation within the family that must be welcomed but that adds to the intricacies of family life.

Key issues

- More individual and democratic households inevitably mean that there will be a range of brands within households. Taking a household perspective will be increasingly complex. The shopper (whoever that may be) will be buying multiple brands for different people, for different occasions.
- The strength of the family and continuing links even with adult children suggests new opportunities for products – and particularly financial services – that cater for the whole family. An example might be family cover that spreads risk across the older and younger members (normally benefiting the latter).

Anxiety society

The concerns that parents have and the seriousness with which they approach their responsibilities are also, in part, a reflection of a broader and more pernicious social development that adds to the uncertainties of life – the emergence of what one might call the 'anxiety society'. It is no coincidence that in a complicated society we worry more, and about more trivial things. But it is also the case that having more worries in turn makes life more complicated. So, the concerns about diet and health, illness and disease, security and safety, for ourselves and our children and loved ones, generate a bewildering set of decisions that have to be made on a daily basis. Even though most risks are smaller (longevity would not be increasing so dramatically if this was not the case), we are more aware of them, often exaggerating their real threat. In such a situation, how do we know what is the right action to take? How can we keep informed enough to make sensible and rational decisions? The answer is we cannot – which is why consumer behaviour tends to be increasingly volatile and irrational. To the extent that people do try to keep informed or make rational decisions about health, safety or other perceived risks they might be exposed to, it also means that life feels more stressful, more convoluted.

Key issues

■ It seems inevitable that there will be increasing volatility in consumer behaviour as scares and anxieties undermine consumer trust in products and the pronouncements of experts. With less rational consumers, planning becomes much harder and fluctuations in market shares and attitudes to products and brands likely to be greater.

■ Doing whatever you can to build trust in your brand – by simple product delivery or being a citizen brand – will help. But, having crisis control mechanisms in place – procedures and people – will also be important.

Complicated times – understanding time and priorities

It is these complexities that put added pressure on that increasingly precious commodity for many people – time. In a 'have it all' world – where our ambitions and aspirations are almost unlimited, where there are more choices and worries that require us to make our own decisions and where we have to pay attention to managing our social and cultural capital – it is inevitable that people are constrained by the limits of time. There are only 24 hours in a day. The reality of wanting to do more things and having more choices and the feeling of stress about more, and more complex, decision-making inevitably increases the perception of time pressure.

There is no easy solution to this conundrum – wanting to have it all but not having the time to do so – but understanding it and the inevitable trade-offs people have to make is critical for business and public sector service providers. And it is much more complex than merely reducing the time spent on an activity. We prefer the concept of 'time trade-offs', which considers all the emotional, physical and social benefits and costs that people weigh up when making their consumption and lifestyle choices. Understanding this provides immense insight into how you can, and cannot, relieve life's complications.

Key issues

- Most time is tradable – you could be doing something else. As *the* most precious commodity for the affluent majority who have some degree of financial discretion, time-value for one activity is traded off against time-value in another. As such, everyone is a competitor now.

- The key questions are: are you solving people's problems? Are you putting them in control? Or are you giving them 'time' space? If you are doing any of these, you will succeed.

- The perceived pace of time is important too. Feeling busy and hectic instils two polarized reactions: a desire to solve things quickly (convenience) and a yearning to slow things down. Where are you placed? What are you trying to do? Are you a slow brand associated with reflection, relaxation and regeneration – like Cadbury's Flake or Champneys Health Resort or a golf club – or a fast one that is buzzy, convenient and problem solving – like Vodafone or McCain Micro Chips or easyCar car rental?

NAVIGATING A COMPLEX WORLD

Whether you are a business, a government agency or an individual this increasing complexity in life, and the impacts it threatens, have immense implications. It affects how you operate as a company, an organization or in your day-to-day life.

From a business perspective it raises questions about, and points to the benefits of, mass customization and choice management tools. It also reinforces the potential value of brands and the importance of building trust in them. It explains why communications technologies have been such a success (the importance of social capital and managing complexity) and why certain new technologies will, and will not, succeed. It highlights the assistance people will need in the future, suggesting opportunities in such areas as self-help, personal development and advisory services. It clarifies why as individualism grows and complexity advances so consumers become less segmentable and less predictable and points to ways of addressing this. And it shows how an understanding of the complex relationship between such complicated lives and time will be a major aspect of success in the future.

Whatever way you look at it, understanding people's 'complicated lives' today is a critical business issue – perhaps in the 21st century, the most critical one of all.

CHAPTER 2

THE NEW INDIVIDUALISM

*I*t is an undeniable fact that we live in a more individualized world. People think of themselves more as individuals than members of a given, restrictive group such as a social class, a profession or a geographical entity (restrictive being the critical word here). Consequently they expect products and services that are moulded to their own needs rather than those of a broad, amorphous group.

But why is this happening? Does it necessarily mean that people are becoming more selfish and less interested in being members of groups or engaging with communities? The answer to this question is a resounding 'no' – as we shall see in the next chapter. This is why we call this the 'new' individualism – it is not about the individual as opposed to society, but about how people's sense of identity is increasingly complex, nuanced, and self-aware[1]. The 'self' is now something we seek to understand and express, not something we simply accept. This raises difficult issues for individuals as well as our companies and public services who are still struggling to escape the historical legacy of mass provision.

The harsh realities of existence have, in the past, constrained what people could and could not do. Merely to survive, people lived in close-knit groups, accepted structures and roles and did what was expected of them. They followed the behaviours and lifestyles that were dictated by tradition, mores or authority figures. Of course there were rebels – history is littered with stories of individuals heroically fighting against the constraints of their position, class or religion. (That the image of the individual struggling against rigid systems has been such an enduring and successful one is surely a testament to the underlying feelings of society.) But, for the majority, the grouping you were born into (or in some instances made your way into) greatly determined the way you behaved and, particularly, what you consumed.

But this has changed, as the data in Figure 2.1 show. The chart plots the responses for different birth cohorts (for example, those born between 1946 and 1955) and tracks their responses to the question 'It's more important to fit in than to be different from

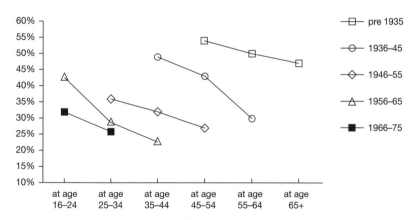

Figure 2.1 No longer happy just to fit in. Proportion agreeing that 'It's more important to fit in than to be different from other people' by different birth cohorts.

Source: nVision, Future Foundation/Taylor Nelson Sofres.

other people') at different periods of time. So, those born between 1946 and 1955 were aged 25–34 in 1980 and their responses at that time (around a third agreed with the statement) have duly been recorded. As we can see, not only is each successive cohort (what we might call a generation) less inclined to 'fit in' than the previous one, but people in every age group have become more individualistic over the last twenty years. Over the course of that time we have moved from a predominant belief that we should 'fit in' to one where we would rather be different: individualism is now a defining feature of social and consumer behaviour.

It is clear from what we have said that the declining influence of traditional institutions is a major cause of the growth in individualism and we discuss the factors driving this in the next chapter. But more important than this is the simple fact that people are richer – people just have greater economic resources to pick and choose what they themselves want to own and to do.

THE AFFLUENT SOCIETY

Incomes have grown enormously since the Second World War. In Britain household disposable income rose three-fold in real terms between the early 1950s and the start of the new millennium – an average increase of 2.5% per annum. This has had a major impact on the material aspects of people's existence. Televisions, telephones, washing machines, refrigerators and central heating are the norm. Not only can many people afford holidays, many take more than one a year. Increasingly the destinations are overseas and to ever more exotic places. This reflects the critical aspect of the rise in affluence – that more and more of it can be used for effectively discretionary spending. Nowadays, new appliances reach high penetration levels in relatively short periods of time simply because people have the spare cash to be able to buy new products that arrive on the market.

People are not only better off in income terms (Figure 2.2) but in assets too with the total net wealth held by British households having doubled in real terms over the last 15 years to reach over £4,000 billion[2]. There is little doubt that we live in an affluent society.

The term 'affluent society' was first coined by J. K. Galbraith more than forty years ago[3]. Then, for the first time in history, spending became discretionary in the sense that many people could begin to consider purchasing items beyond those of basic subsistence (like food) or security (a home). This was hugely important in the analysis of economic development and of marketing and branding in particular. Consumers were so undiscriminating and so eager to buy product that it has been said that in 1950s America 'you could market dog poop in a paper bag if you had half a brain'[4]. But as the level of discretionary income has increased, so too has the impact on consumer attitudes and behaviour: the implications of affluence have changed. The term may be an old one, but the concept of an affluent society (albeit an amended

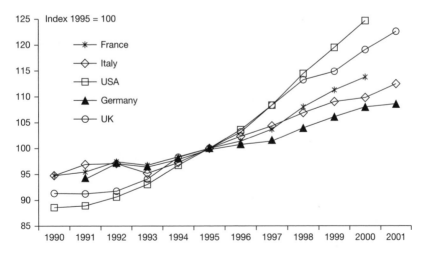

Figure 2.2 Household disposable income growth. Index of disposable income in real terms for selected EU countries and the USA (1995 = 100).

Source: OECD 2002/nVision.

one) remains crucial to understanding the relationship between consumers, products, services and brands.

At around the same time as Galbraith was writing, Abraham Maslow was articulating his theory of a hierarchy of needs[5]. In this, Maslow argued that as societies develop, so their citizens move up what he called a 'hierarchy of needs'. So, in primitive societies the critical issue was food and other basic sustenance required just to live. As societies develop security (safety and roof over the head) becomes more important, then after that what Maslow called 'socialization' – a need for community and belonging. The final stages are self-esteem and self-actualization. The former is associated with lifestyles focusing on status-driven consumption or what some commentators have labelled 'competitive consumption', while the latter is less concerned with appearance and more with personal development, quality of life and with wider concerns. This was amazingly prescient as research suggests that at that point in time there were few people in the 'self-actualized' phase. Now, however, significant numbers are[6].

Fast-forward these two theories forty-odd years, adjust and amend them accordingly, and we have a powerful proposition: that for most citizens in the industrialized world, affluence has reached such levels and consumers have such a degree of discretion that people have developed a fundamentally different set of needs and expectations. This manifests itself in a number of ways.

A MORE DEMANDING AND MARKETING-LITERATE CONSUMER

Being better off gives consumers confidence – specifically confidence to be different. The new affluent society promotes individualism. This has important implications for brands, since they are less about 'what I have' and more about differentiation and 'how I am'. The consumption, or refusal, of particular goods has reflected

aspects of personal identity since time immemorial. But today's consumer has so much more discretion, so many more qualities and
meanings to consider, and attitudes to the self and self-expression
that are increasingly sophisticated (as we discuss later). It is quite
hard to imagine what a typical consumer of the 1950s would have
made of the idea that you can 'express yourself' through normal
consumption. Consumption habits (and particularly brand choice)
not only tell us something about people now, they can suggest very
specific elements of identity, and people's grasp of such distinctions
is growing, at the same time as the ability to define and discuss
them.

But this presents dangers to companies and brands as growing
affluence also gives consumers confidence to be more demanding
in their dealings with companies. The affluent majority know
they can pick and choose, argue and pontificate over what are,
effectively, non-essential items. They expect and demand more of
companies. More than this, they are incredibly marketing-literate.

To understand modern consumers it is essential to realize how
much the specific relationship between them and marketers has
changed, and how much consumers have developed a critical
understanding of this relationship. Two generations ago, discretionary spending and sophisticated mass marketing were young.
But now they are phenomena that the great majority have grown
up with. Even 12-year-olds now know that advertised goods
may be so much dog poop in the paper bag of branding. Many
of us now learn anti-marketing counter-narratives, not least
from parents keen to moderate the expensive effects of child-
focused advertising. Even where this does not happen, a critical
attitude to marketing is now almost a logical necessity. The sheer
volume and semiotic richness of modern marketing creates a
distance from it – there is no way a modern consumer can understand one marketing message as just that (and so reject or ignore
the offer), and then absorb another with complete naivety. The
more brands want to be meaningful, want to be a part of our

self-representation, the more we are bound to think twice before letting them be.

The more politically engaged manifestations of this response to marketing have been much discussed, not least in the bible of the anti-marketing movement *No Logo*[7], but they are not our focus here. Indeed, partly because of the fall-out from September 11, partly because of the massive internal contradictions of the anti-globalization movement, some commentators are now pondering its 'death'[8]. However, multinationals cannot breathe a sigh of relief. The assault on marketing contained in the thinking of the movement, and central to its appeal to the affluent young radicals of the west, is grounded in this critical distance in the population as a whole. The inevitable reflexive response to two generations of day-to-day experience of mass marketing has a far more profound influence than the agitators who have recently attempted to harness this impact to an anti-corporate agenda. This is not to downplay the role of the political movement in setting the media agenda and voicing a powerful moral critique of big business, but rather to remind us that the 'critical' consumers are the mass, not the minority. The really complex, nuanced, and commercially important responses to brands and marketing may be found in the consumerism/identity politics of people who might still buy Calvin Klein before Naomi Klein.

SEEKING FULFILMENT AND EXPERIENCES – THE LURE OF CULTURAL CAPITAL

This complexity of consumerism is heightened by the fact that what people want to consume is changing. Higher incomes allow consumers to seek new 'meanings' consistent with Maslow's self-actualization concept. First, people are more concerned about wider issues such as the environment, animal rights or third world employment practices. In part, of course, this merely reflects the fact that people can afford to worry about such issues – when you are struggling to pay for even basic foods for your family you are unlikely to be overly concerned about whether products are environmentally friendly. But it also reflects a search for a wider meaning and sense of worth beyond material possessions. We will not dwell on this here, not least because one of us has already written a book – *Citizen Brands*[9] – on the growing importance of this issue in consumer behaviour and the perception of companies. All we will point out is that such a 'politicization' of consumption clearly makes life more complicated not only for companies trying to understand and anticipate the hotchpotch of concerns that any individual consumer might have but also for consumers themselves as they contemplate whether a product or service is reliable, properly priced and satisfies their needs and whether it is 'good' too.

A second aspect of self-actualization is that people increasingly seek 'fulfilment' (admittedly a rather ill-defined concept). In the Future Foundation's nVision research a question asks respondents about their main wish in life (from a preset list of five options). 'To fulfil yourself' is now the number one wish with 40% choosing this, up from 20% twenty years ago (Figure 2.3).

This is the driving force behind the shift from spending on material goods to spending on services and experiences. At one level this just means increased spending on things like holidays, eating out, theatre and cinema but at its more extreme it includes 'special' experiences like white water rafting, spending a weekend at a health spa or driving around a Formula One racetrack. It also includes added-value entertainment, the 'shopping as theatre', that retail increasingly seems to offer. Our research in Britain shows that the proportion of the population that feels a strong or moderate need for 'new experiences' has increased by over a quarter (from 46% to 58%) in the last 20 years[10]. Crucially, an analysis of different birth cohorts shows that each new generation is more interested in experiences than previous ones.

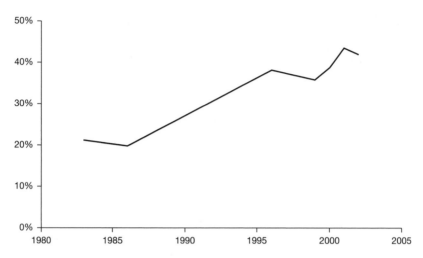

Figure 2.3 Desperately seeking fulfilment. Proportion choosing 'to be able to fulfil yourself' as their one wish from a list of five.

Source: nVision, Future Foundation/Taylor Nelson Sofres.

This does not mean that materialism has been banished – most people still do not have as much money or possessions as they might like – rather that other factors are becoming important too. A complex balancing act takes place between consumers' desire to exploit or express economic status and their wider set of interests, concerns and perceptions of themselves as individuals. And it is this that is behind the shift from 'conspicuous' to 'inconspicuous' consumption[11] since the 1980s.

SELF-EXPRESSION AND 'INCONSPICUOUS' CONSUMPTION

Certainly, our own research is consistent with a shift away from more ostentatious consumption. Figure 2.4 shows how between the early 1980s and the current day the proportions of people in Britain concerned about 'having the best money can buy' or

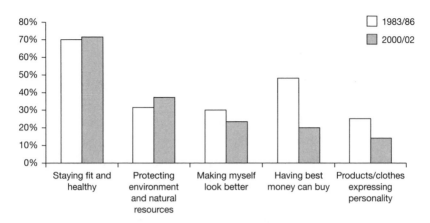

Figure 2.4 What concerns people. Proportion saying they are concerned.

Source: nVision, Future Foundation/Taylor Nelson Sofres.

'products/clothes that express my personality' have declined significantly. On the other hand, consumers remained highly concerned about retaining the state of their health while those expressing concern for the environment (an indicator of beliefs and self-actualization) has risen.

But the relationship between social, cultural or intellectual competence (human capital) and wealth (or at least the potential to get it) remains at the heart of social status and hence consumption patterns. This is no less true because the cultured, educated classes consider it 'bad taste' to make this connection explicit. Partly this denial exists because the link to wealth is less clear for those *directly* employed in the intellectual and 'culture' industries, and especially the younger ones, who tend to earn less than their counterparts in more directly commercial sectors, and so emphasize a scheme of values that downplays economic wealth. Partly it is because those with a greater abundance of human capital inevitably wish to explain their dominance by inherent intellectual sophistication rather than an advantage that is merely purchased[12]. This denial is one explanation for the move to a more 'inconspicuous' mode of consumption. But there is a 'game' being played out here, too – there are moves and counter-moves in the history of status and self-expression.

To clarify, let us sketch a somewhat simplified 'potted history' of inconspicuous consumption. Between the 1950s and 1980s a massive range of consumer goods came within the economic reach of the newly affluent majority of workers. The ownership of new cars, white goods, and high quality clothing thus became a marker of prosperity that separated the mainstream from the unemployed and very low-paid underclass. Those from the higher social strata (and the marketing community) began to realize this in the 1980s, and ostentatious spending on big ticket consumer goods was soon recognized as a marker of relatively *lower* social status. So they have responded by finding subtler modes of distinction, drawing upon the new array of intellectual resources at their disposal.

Don't get us wrong. We are not suggesting that people no longer care about what they look like – after all, consumer spending on beauty and cosmetic products is higher than ever. And, our research across Europe shows that more people still agree than disagree that 'the brand of clothing I wear is important to me' (with interesting differences between countries[13]). It just seems that they are also likely to use aspects other than their appearance as a means of differentiating themselves from others. The 'new' individualism is more about people's beliefs, values, expertise and experiences than about what they own, do or wear and personal appearance actually provides a good example. Since at least 1995, women's spending in Britain on cosmetics and toiletries has been shifting from 'ostentatious' cosmetics such as eye shadow, lipstick and nail varnish, to 'stealthy' cosmetics (whose effects are hard to distinguish from 'natural' beauty) such as moisturizer, shampoo, and hair dye[14]. At the same time, concern with 'health' has risen, and gyms have become particularly popular with women over the last decade. Few people would put a figure on it, but it is no coincidence that for women, being obese is almost as strongly related to poverty as dishwasher ownership is linked to wealth. You don't have to be a sociologist to sense these distinctions. So, we are not less concerned with physical enhancement, but somehow it must be more natural, more 'true' to our selves and our lifestyles.

When it comes to possessions, expensive clothing, along with so many other goods, no longer distinguishes the affluent mass from the very affluent minority. There are only three routes to take in response. First is to buy *very* expensive consumer products, or disproportionately expensive, high-quality or hand-made goods. It is certainly true that high-end luxury brands do not appear to have suffered as a result of inconspicuous consumption. For example, Nokia has recently set up a subsidiary – Vertu – to make luxury phones for the wealthy that 'will come in a variety of precious metals, boasts a sapphire face and leather sides'[15].

Second, our purchases can demonstrate not so much our ability to afford them, but sensitivity to broader aesthetic or ethical agendas. The need for more subtle demonstrations of social status has partly fuelled the sales of ethical products. Third, we might reject the relation of certain categories of goods to our self-expression altogether. The ability to distinguish good-quality, 'natural' and 'authentic' products from crudely marketed status symbols becomes more important to people.

All of this not only makes life more complicated for companies trying to sell their goods and services to consumers because their motivations are less 'visible' but it makes life more complex for individuals too. With, as we argue in the next chapter, less of a 'package deal' in terms of how you should behave as a consumer, things are inevitably less clear-cut – building your own identity through experiences and learning is not only more time-consuming but, in a way, more lonely too. This is one of the reasons why people are still concerned about the groups they belong to, the communities they are part of and the families and friends they are increasingly turning to for advice.

WANTING IT ALL

Part of the reason why the new individualism is so demanding on people's time is that not only do we seek more of an experiential life, not only do we have the economic means to participate in a wider range of activities, but we just expect to be able to have it all. We have become greedy for life and its experiences. It is this, rather than longer working hours that is creating the perceived time pressures of modern life.

The problem is that not only do people expect a successful and rewarding career but they also look forward to being great parents and having a happy family life while at the same time participating in an ever widening and varied range of leisure pursuits. This is as true for men as it is for women in the sense that men increasingly take their parenting roles seriously and are spending ever more time on childcare. We discuss some of the intricacies and implications of gender and family responsibilities in Chapters 8 and 9, while we consider the time issues themselves in Chapter 11. Here, we will restrict ourselves to making the point that increasingly, as part of the new individualism, it is our activities, rather than our possessions, that define who we are. This, in part, drives the desire to want it all but inevitably it also brings complexity. Managing life (as we note in Chapter 4) is potentially more complex than managing material goods.

There is an added degree of intricacy that makes the life of the marketer so much more difficult. This is that as part of wanting to have and fulfil all these different roles people become, in effect, not just one identity, but *multiple* identities. Understanding who someone is – concerned mother, dynamic executive, playful socialite about town – at a given point in time can be extremely difficult for organizations trying to assess and address that individual's needs. Even individuals themselves might be forgiven for sometimes getting confused.

AGE AND INDIVIDUALISM

Finally, there is a neurological aspect to the growing individualism. In her book *The Private Life of the Brain*[16] Professor Susan Greenfield makes the point that our brains adapt continuously to whatever we may learn or experience in everyday living. Thus, each individual's neurological networks develop in the light of each new day's stimulation. In this way, we develop our own personal view and analysis of the world. The obvious conclusion from this is that an ageing population (which most advanced economies have) is likely to be a more individualistic one too.

This is not to say that older people might not become more 'set' in their own individual ways, thus creating another paradox of the modern era: that people are more individualistic yet more conservative. This might explain why we can observe around the world the multiple developments of resistance to change, increasing expectation of individual treatment and more demanding consumers. People *know* what they want and expect to receive it. Our research shows that it is younger people who are the opposite: accepting of change but more interested in group/clan solutions (see, for example, their much greater interest in what is perceived by society to be fashionable and their attachment to brands). All this is consistent with Greenfield's thesis:

> My particular definition of mind will be that it is the seething morass of cell circuitry that has been configured by personal experiences and is constantly being updated as we live out each moment. So important factors in making you, a human being, the person you are, are the personal experiences that you alone have had – what amounts to your memories .... The personalisation of the physical brain is driven not so much by genes as by individual experiences.[17]

Readers should recognize that the resistance to change we refer to is not necessarily directed to consumer choice in the form of loyalty. Here, it seems that the expectation of delivery (the more demanding element of experienced consumers) outweighs the need for stability (the resistance to change). Analysis of our own consumer research data suggests loyalty to brands is no higher for those aged over 35 than for younger groups. The only exception is the oldest age group, aged 65 and over, but we strongly suspect (from other research) that this is a function of their upbringing (born before the Second World War) rather than the result of age as such. Thus, an older, more individualized and more fragmented population may not even deliver companies the comfort of stable customer bases.

MANAGING IN A WORLD OF INDIVIDUALS

So, the individualism that arises from increased economic and social discretion brings with it a range of complications. That is not to say that individualism is a bad thing – we believe it is a liberating force – but that as a society we are still grappling with how to embrace it in a way that satisfies us without burning us out. The main problem is that the phenomenon makes choice harder. There is simply more to choose from, as we show in Chapter 7, and no longer a simple, 'follow-my-leader' mechanism for deciding. If we want our own thing, we have to choose it. At the same time, we expect so much more, not only in terms of possessions but life choices too. We want to do what we see others doing but we want to do it our own way. We want to have it all but by a different route to everyone else. This creates a whole range of dilemmas. We want a job that matches our needs and expectations, we buy clothes that show we are not part of the crowd (or, if it is to show we are part of a crowd, that it is a small exclusive one), we seek holidays that suit us, we want to design our homes in a way that expresses our uniqueness. But how can you make the right choices, particularly in those areas that require specialist expertise? And how, on earth, do we have enough time to buy and do all these things?

This paradox provides the clue to the way forward. For individuals, the key is *prioritization* and *balance*. People will have to accept that while they can indeed have it all, they can only do so by reining back on expectations. Patently, not everything can be done to the maximum, all at the same time. One simple way to do this is to take more of a life-course approach to planning – something people have always done (I will go round the world in 5 years' time) – but this may have to be done in a more consciously planned way in the future. But the big challenge is for companies and public services who have an immense potential to provide the substantial help that is required. Understanding work–life balance and embracing flexible working throughout a career are obvious starting points. Another is simply making processes and systems easier. Recognize that people will want personalized solutions and look at how products and services can be customized to individual needs (mass customization). These last two points present a particular challenge to public services – providing universal services that are personalized to each citizen (obvious examples being health and education).

Providing advice on both life choices (for example, what skills do I need, when should I buy my first house?) and product and service variations is a further opportunity. This should be a growing activity for both the commercial and not-for-profit sectors. And, companies, as we discuss further in Chapter 7, can do a lot in promoting brands as tools for navigating the maelstrom of choice. Finally, we should not forget the potential for technology to ease the irritations of life while releasing time from more mundane tasks for more fulfilling ones. One of the big stories of the last 50 years has been how much the time spent on household chores has been reduced, allowing us to do more in other areas. The lesson from the past is that people have readily devoured that time on a range of activities: more shopping, more leisure, more dedicated time with children. In fact, they have tried to do more than the released time allowed. That is why life seems busier, that is why life is more complicated, and that is why consumers will readily embrace solutions to the pressures that individualism brings. Such solutions include mass customization in various forms and elements of branding and service delivery. We expand on these in our final chapter.

CHAPTER 3

THE ROUTELESS SOCIETY

As we noted in the last chapter, one of the major factors that has unleashed the urge to be more individualistic has been a decline in the hold that society's institutions have over people. It is not, as we will show, as simple as a decline in trust in such bodies, more that there is less deference towards them. The result is that people are less bound by what governments, the church, the media and even scientists tell them is the right way to behave. There are fewer external 'givens' or 'signposts' to guide people through their lives. In such a 'routeless' society, there is much more emphasis on developing one's own life strategies; there is more choice; and inevitably, things seem less settled and less straightforward. Here, then, is another complication of the modern world.

This development is not necessarily a bad thing (although many commentators suggest it is) since it is potentially liberating and empowering, but it inevitably creates huge challenges for both governments and business. What these are, and the implications that arise from them, is what this chapter is about. But before considering these, let us look at the evidence that the life-shaping influence of institutions is declining.

THE CHANGING INFLUENCE OF INSTITUTIONS

It has become fashionable to suggest that there is declining trust in institutions like the medical profession, government or the church[1]. The World Economic Forum at Davos in January 2003 ran under the title 'Building Trust'. According to the Forum:

> The string of corporate scandals in 2002 contributed to the serious undermining of trust . . . Trust *has been eroded* far beyond the corporate sector.[2] [Our emphasis]

Indeed, some have argued that many organizations and professions are becoming less important – even irrelevant – to society and individuals. Yet, there is in fact little evidence that we trust institutions less or rate them as less important. The World Economic Forum based its views on a survey that showed that some institutions had low levels of trust. But maybe that has always been the case? To know whether trust is declining we need to look at how opinions have changed over time.

In Britain, the opinion polling organization MORI has been asking the general public for 20 years whether they trust certain professions to tell the truth. As Figure 3.1 illustrates there has, in fact, been little change over that period. Certainly, some professions have had dips as a result of revelations about their conduct – the series of miscarriages of justice that came to light in Britain around 1990 led to the rating for judges declining slightly and concerns about sexual abuse by the clergy in the mid-1990s had a similar impact. Both recovered in the late 1990s only to have

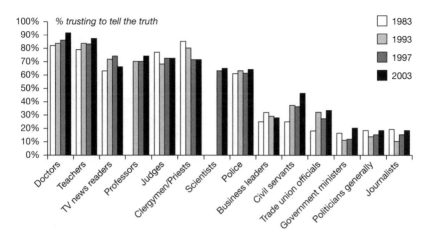

Figure 3.1 Public trust in UK professionals. Question asked: For each of the following different types of people, would you tell me if you generally trust them to tell the truth, or not?

Source: MORI.

fallen back again in the light of more problems since 2000. Interestingly, some professions have seen their ratings increase – notably public servants like doctors, teachers and those in the civil service. Even government ministers are at a higher level than they were in the 1980s and 1990s (bearing in mind that this was written before it was clear what effect, if any, had been caused by the crisis over Iraq). Recently, there has been a slight decline in trust for business leaders. After the pro-business zeitgeist of the 1980s when, remember, corporate greed was good[3], the rating reached a high point in the early 1990s when a third of the population trusted corporate heads to tell the truth. Even at this level, it was hardly a ringing endorsement of the perceived integrity of business, yet by 2003 this rating had fallen back, but not as much as might have been expected given the scandals in corporate America in 2001–2002. Scientists – who were first included in the survey in 1997 – had two-thirds trusting them in 2003, showing little change over six years despite all the concerns and bad publicity surrounding genetically modified foods and the like. Why then is there such talk about a decline in trust? A cynic might note that much of this comes from journalists who, on this measure, and amongst these professions, are the least trusted of all.

Figure 3.1 looked at professionals being trusted *to tell the truth*. What about just generally trusting a profession or organization? Here, the European data in Figure 3.2 present a similar pattern. Admittedly it is over a shorter time span but general trust in a range of institutions is unchanged over a five-year period when it became received wisdom that there was a crisis of confidence in our institutions. There is no real evidence from Europe that trust is declining in institutions. Admittedly, people seem not to trust in the church quite as much as they once did, but across all the categories included here, the ratings have generally risen.

There are, of course differences between countries in which institutions are trusted or not. In Britain, for example, there is significantly lower trust in the press (but not television or radio),

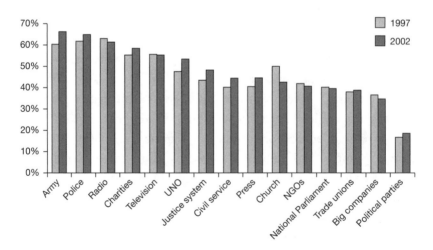

Figure 3.2 Trust in European institutions. 'Do you tend to trust or not the following institutions?' – % saying tend to trust.

Source: Eurobarometer/nVision Europe.

big business and, unsurprisingly, the European Union. But the degree of change, or rather the lack of it, is consistent across the continent.

What about the United States? After all, much of the discourse about declining institutions comes from there[4]. Figure 3.3 gives the results of a somewhat differently worded question asked by Harris Polls. Here the question is whether people think an occupation has a high level of prestige[5]. The question was first asked in 1977 and across the occupations there was a fall between 1977 and 1982. Since then, however, things have, on the whole, been pretty constant. Yes, there has been a big increase for the military (something that is evident in Europe too) and for teachers. This has been matched by a significant fall for lawyers. But, overall, across the professions there has been a slight increase over the 20-year period.

The organizers of the World Economic Forum were surprised that governments and large companies were not much trusted and that armies were. They should not have been, since it seems highly likely that this has always been the case. Some institutions are not trusted, but looking back over the recent past, it appears that they have never been. The dynamic here is not a decline in trust but a lack of improvement in trust – an important distinction.

So from looking at a range of questions across a range of countries there hardly seems to be the collapse of trust that many analysts have insisted upon. Where there are declines, there are often specific explanations for them. For example, Harris notes that the sex abuse scandals in America have dented the clergy's position in the last year[6].

Business generally and business leaders are under some pressure but not perhaps as much as might be thought post-Enron. But other surveys do point to an increasing cynicism about business behaviour. In a special report, 'Scandals in corporate America', *Business Week* pointed out that 'public confidence in Big Business is at its lowest since 1981, according to the latest Gallup Poll'[7].

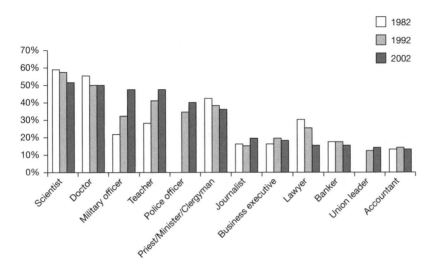

Figure 3.3 Occupational prestige in the United States. Is the occupation of 'very great prestige, considerable prestige, some prestige or hardly any prestige at all'? Proportion saying 'very great'. (Note: 'Police officer' was previously worded as 'Policeman' and 'Business executive' as 'Businessman'.)

Source: Harris Polls/Harris Interactive.

It is important that business in particular recognizes that not only are consumers becoming ever more cynical about its behaviour and activities but that it never was particularly well thought of in the first place. There was not some golden era when the general public just loved corporations, so there is not some easy mechanism for returning to higher levels of respect. As others have pointed out, addressing this is a major challenge for the corporate sector, which probably requires a re-engagement with society and its citizens[8].

We can see, then, that the problem is not so much a decline in trust. Neither could we say these bodies have become irrelevant. The issues facing the world, whether they be terrorism, racial or religious tension or economic policy and globalization, are as difficult now as at any point in history. The role of institutions in how these issues develop – and their power to influence the direction of change – is as important as ever. This is especially true for governments – politics still do matter – but also for religious groups and professional bodies (think of the role of scientists in the forthcoming bio-genetic debates that will inevitably take place). Business has its role too. But, and this is the critical point we want to make, the ability of such institutions to determine what people do is reduced. They can affect the environment that people operate in, but are less able to control what individuals themselves might do. Lifestyles can no longer be determined by state, religious, family or class dictates.

In part this reflects the growing confidence of individuals that we discussed in the last chapter and with it an increasing reluctance to accept without question the 'packaged' offer of a large and distant institution. But there is an interesting counter-point to this decline in deference – the growing influence of more personal authorities like family, friends and work colleagues. Contrary to general claims about a decline in family, community or friendship networks they are, in fact, becoming more influential in some aspects of people's lives (see also Chapter 5 for more discussion on some of the myths about the family). In this sense there is what might be called a 'personalization of authority'.

This has very important implications for business since it changes the validity and value of the endorsements from, or associations with, a variety of society's institutions. It should be no surprise that advertising no longer uses the scientist in a white coat to confer legitimacy on a product since, as we showed earlier, although we might generally trust scientists we no longer defer to them. What is needed now is advertising that reflects our lives or the people and lifestyles that we can personally relate to. This is another way of viewing the shift in the nature of advertising from persuasion (which focuses on the functional superiority of a product) to involvement (which highlights the empathy, or associations between, a product and the consumer) that has been identified by, amongst others, Mike Hall[9].

THE PERSONALIZATION OF AUTHORITY (AND THE RE-EMERGENCE OF COMMUNITY?)

Evidence of the importance of 'closer' authorities is shown in Figure 3.4 where family and friends are seen as more important in affecting purchase decisions than any of the other potential sources of advice. Of course, there are differences between countries – differences that may depend on anything from overall consumer confidence to stronger traditional family structures to national marketing traditions. For example, four out of five Irish consumers consult 'friends and relatives' compared with just over half of Belgians (whose most popular information source was advertising leaflets). TV is an unsurprisingly important source of information in many countries but 'friends and relatives' score higher than TV in 10 of the 15 countries surveyed.

But it is interesting to note that across Europe 'friends and relatives' have a greater influence on the young. If young people,

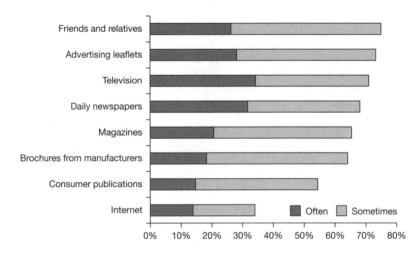

Figure 3.4 Information sources used in purchase decisions. Proportion of Europeans saying they 'often' or 'sometimes' consult the categories listed on the figure before making a purchase decision.

Source: Flash Eurobarometer/nVision Europe.

spurred on by the new technologies they are more likely to have access to, take their current sources of influence with them into later life, the personalization of authority, and thus the potency of word-of-mouth based marketing strategies, will become increasingly powerful.

In any case, some of our own research in Britain shows that the influence of these 'personalized' authorities is growing. In this research, first conducted in 1997 and repeated in 2001, we asked who were most influential in the development of people's views on social and environmental problems. As can be seen from Figure 3.5, while the proportion saying they were influenced by friends, family and work colleagues has gone up, for institutions like government, the media or the church it has gone down quite significantly.

This has important implications:

■ This personalization of authority allows people increasingly to define their own networks of authority, making them much harder to understand, predict and segment.

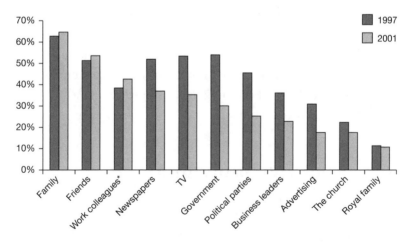

Figure 3.5 Sources of influence. Proportion saying that the categories shown on the figure influence their views about social and environmental problems 'a lot' or 'somewhat'. *Base: only those who have a job.

Source: *The Responsible Organisation*[10], BT/Future Foundation; nVision.

- It is encouraging more contact and connectivity directly between individuals – something that is aided by, and encouraging, the new communications technologies (see Chapter 6).
- Also, who one's contacts are – who one can trust and rely upon for good advice – becomes more important. The connections you have and the capabilities and influence of your friends and families – your 'social capital' – becomes critical.
- As such, word-of-mouth becomes a more important factor – and understanding this and trying to influence it is more important for organizations.
- It is leading to a revival, or at the very least a maintenance, of the more personal institutions in society – family, friendship networks and local communities.

It is on this last point that many commentators are misled in their analysis, since the argument that society is breaking down and communities are dissolving is, to our mind, over-exaggerated to say the least. Take, for example, the views of one of the most prominent advocates of this theory – the American academic Robert Putnam. In his controversial and widely read book *Bowling Alone*[11], Putnam claims that social capital (which he defines as the 'connections among individuals – social networks and the norms and reciprocity and trustworthiness that arise from them') is being eroded. He argues that people are becoming increasingly disconnected from family, friends and neighbours.

COLLABORATIVE INDIVIDUALISTS

But Putnam has a growing number of critics, us among them. Richard Florida, a professor of regional economic development at Carnegie Mellon University, summarizes many of these critiques in his book *The Rise of the Creative Class*[12]. The main arguments against Putnam are:

1. His definition of social capital is based on old-style, declining organizations (like the bowling leagues of the book's title) but that new organizations and activities are developing to replace these (which because they are new cannot be measured over the period of 30 years that Putnam considers).
2. That in any case his analysis is wrong. For example, Putnam claims that volunteering in America has declined but others have reanalysed his data and claim there is little evidence of this[13].
3. That the old-style, social capital, being based on more rigid and restrictive institutions, is not appropriate for the modern world and the modern economy. Indeed, Florida's research suggests they are a constraint to economic growth: 'Traditional notions of what it means to be a close, cohesive community and society tend to inhibit economic growth and innovation.'[14]

Our research in Britain certainly does not support the contention that there is an erosion of social capital. For example, people are eating out more, not less and visiting friends in their homes more often than they did 30 or 40 years ago; and the proportion of people volunteering has increased[15]. Research by sociologist Peter Willmott amongst families in the East End of London found that although family members were more dispersed than they had been in the 1950s, there had been little change in the volume of contact by the 1990s thanks to the introduction of that new technology, the telephone:

> So in this one locality at least [Bethnal Green], taking the telephone into account, the falls in co-residence and in propinquity had not led to the expected reduction in contact between parents and their adult children.[16]

This research is supported by a British longitudinal study that is tracking the lives of a sample of people born in 1946, 1958 and 1970[17]. It shows that despite the physical dispersal of extended families that has taken place and the potentially disruptive influence of divorce and relationship breakdown, family contact (and support) remains high. As the authors note: 'there was no indication that the more recent cohorts [those born in 1970 as opposed to those born in 1958] had less contact with their own mothers and fathers'. Perhaps of more interest and of surprise to the researchers was the finding that the degree of emotional closeness between middle-aged adults and their parents was increasing. Figure 3.6 shows this happening for both sexes and that it applies to both their mothers and fathers. The biggest difference between the generations has been the rise in those saying they were very close.

So it seems that one result of a decline in the influence and relevance of traditional institutions and in old-style community activity is that closer, more personal attachments become more important. Surely, then, it is a fairly futile exercise to hark back

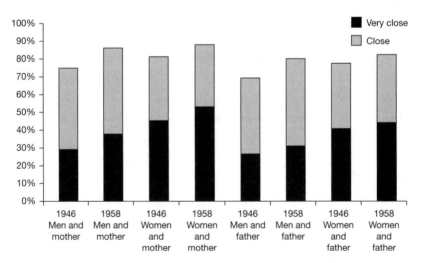

Figure 3.6 Growing emotional closeness within families. Proportion of people in their early forties saying they are very close or close to their own parents (those born in 1946 interviewed in 1990; those born in 1958 interviewed in 2000).

Source: *Changing Britain, Changing Lives,* Ferri, Bynner and Wadsworth, 2003[18].

to past times and past institutions. Or to bemoan the demise of forms of social organization that were appropriate then but not only have less relevance now but are actively rejected by individuals. As Richard Florida points out:

> Where old social structures were once nurturing, now they are restricting. Communities that once attracted people now repel them. Our evolving communities and emerging society are marked by greater diversity of friendships, more individualistic pursuits and weaker ties within the community.[19]

What we are witnessing, then, is a more individualized, personal, loose-knit and multi-stranded world – one that Charles Leadbeater has described as a 'personalized society'. Society and communities still exist – as does social capital – but they take a form that embraces the new individualism we have already discussed. Another term Leadbeater uses to describe the phenomenon and that we particularly like is 'collaborative individualists'[20].

The conclusion from this – that people still yearn for, and need some form of community but do not want ones that restrict their individualist desires – is hugely important for both government and business. Many of the problems faced by public services around the world are a reflection of this tension. Nowhere is this more obvious than in Britain's health service, where there is massive public support for a state system but growing disillusionment with its inability to cater for different people's different expectations and needs. Building public services that are individually flexible while at the same time also equitable is a real challenge.

For business, the real opportunities arise from the very fact that there is an interest in new forms of community and there is a need for new anchors of belonging to replace the discarded ones of traditional institutions. Thus:

1. People are still interested in joining organizations that are relevant to their own needs and predilections. Such *communities of*

interest have always existed and always will but they will emerge and evolve in areas that reflect the key concerns and interests of the day. Companies can facilitate this process by creating areas and discussion forums on, for example, their websites. But they can go further as Kimberly-Clark has done with its *Huggies Club* in a number of European countries. This provides advice for parents on a range of child-rearing questions as well as an area where members can discuss issues and a shop where relevant baby products are available. By showing that it recognizes the issues and concerns facing young parents – and creating a community for like-minded people – Kimberly-Clark hopes to build up brand recognition and loyalty. For such initiatives to be successful, there obviously has to be a direct link between the company's products and the community – as with Kimberly-Clark's Huggies nappies (diapers) and the parents of young babies they are targeting.

2. A company's corporate citizenship credentials could also tap into this interest for community. Knowing that a company both understands society and its problems and has a set of inclusive values is attractive to some consumers, specially so if they have a keen interest in, say, environmental issues. In this sense, people shopping at Body Shop are buying into a community.

3. One of the apparent paradoxes in an era of globalization is the growing interest in local communities and affiliations. But in our yearning for belonging, and in an increasingly fragmented world, there seems to be a clear revival of localism. This manifests itself across the world where regions of nation states are seeking ever-greater autonomy. The implications for brands are two-fold. First, be aware of local conditions, cultures and sentiments. Coca-Cola, having found itself increasingly seen as a detached, global monolith, has under CEO Doug Daft decided to 'think local, act local' in an attempt to reconnect to local communities. Second, do not jettison lightly

historic local affiliations and brands – they could provide a useful 'hook' of authenticity in years to come. Heritage is likely to be an increasingly valuable commodity.

4. Finally, and somewhat differently, recognize that an inevitable outcome of a routeless society is a decline in the efficacy of market segmentation – certainly the traditional ones of age and class. Growing individualism and increasing freedom (as the constraints of institutions fade away) mean that variations can be as great within traditional groupings as between them. We discuss elsewhere some of the implications of this (and possible solutions) but illustrate the point here with some special analysis of the Future Foundation's attitudinal data from the last 20 years. This demonstrates that age is becoming a less important indicator of people's beliefs and values with a 16% decline in the difference between older generations (all aged 45+) and the rest of the population. This convergence is apparent across many measures, but especially in relation to individualism and creative self-fulfilment (older people today are significantly more individualistic and more interested in learning than their forebears in 1980, and thus less differentiated from the rest of the population in these respects).

THE GROWING IMPORTANCE OF SOCIAL CAPITAL

There is one final point we want to make about the reduced influence of traditional institutions and the growing importance of 'personal' authorities – the onus this places on who you know and the connections you have. This is why networking really has become more important and particularly in times of rapid change. As management guru Peter Drucker once noted:

> In any community in transition, it is more important whom you know than what you know. That's the right definition of networking.[21]

In a routeless world, the power of your personal connections – whether they are family, friends or work contacts – becomes more important. So do the skills associated with networking: contact management and social and communication abilities. One of the outcomes of this appears to be a growing importance of family background. Research at the Institute for Social and Economic Research at Essex University in Britain suggests that better educated and richer parents are becoming more important in their children's own success by, for example, working the education system better or using their personal contacts in career development or even introductions to potential spouses[22]. Yet another paradox of the modern world is that in a routeless society where there are fewer givens, your parents become more important. Although people are less deferential to their parents they are more needing of their help and assistance.

We discuss this, and the broader issue of human capital, further in the next chapter but here we will just note the potential commercial opportunities in providing the tools that improve networking and build social capital. This might be training in how best to communicate, to technologies that help communication, to helping to create and promote networking forums – sponsoring meetings for example.

LIFE WITHOUT A MAP

Why has the influence of traditional institutions waned? It is because most people want it that way. In this sense, it is a liberating experience. But it clearly can make life more complex. With fewer 'givens', people have less guidance and fewer 'signposts', meaning that they have to plot their own life strategies and more often make their own choices. We discuss some of the implications of this in later chapters: life courses and the need to understand the transitions that people go through in Chapter 5;

the growing anxiety and perceptions of risk that arise from declining deference and the ensuing volatility in Chapter 10; and the specific area of gender relations – as stereotypes break down – in Chapter 8.

We have already highlighted in this chapter some of the commercial implications of a routeless world. Word-of-mouth is more important and hence managing that in whatever ways one can is potentially crucial. In the sense that we have discussed it here, advertising will need to become more personal – the involvement model will be more relevant. And, branding needs to embrace aspects of community, citizenship, locality and heritage.

But there is another obvious opportunity too that also has implications for branding. In a world with fewer givens, consumers are more likely to need, and therefore welcome, help and guidance on what are the right life choices for them in the hurly-burly complexity of modern life. Some of this they will get from non-commercial agencies – public services, charities and consumer organizations. But there is a potentially major role for companies and brands. Since these are life-course critical decisions, trust will be a critical element. Trusted brands that can solve consumers' problems or even run parts of people's lives will prosper. In Chapter 7 we discuss the role of brands in the decision-making processes involved in everyday consumption. Here we are talking about the role of companies and brands in life choices. The potential is there but the execution will be hard since, as we showed earlier, companies do not currently do well on the trust stakes. The challenge is to turn this around and really help people navigate their way through the complexities of a routeless society.

CHAPTER 4

HUMAN CAPITAL AND THE NETWORK SOCIETY

*I*n the last two chapters we have discussed the increased complications in life that arise from the growth of individualism and the decline in deference towards traditional institutions. Two of the outcomes that we have identified – a decline in the importance of traditional segmentation criteria such as social class and a move away from more conspicuous consumption – are both related to an important development in social positioning: the emergence of new forms of what has come to be known as *human capital*. In fact, there is some confusion about what the term actually means[1] and as Professor Jonathan Gershuny rightly says it is to be hoped 'that a more satisfactory terminology emerges'. But here we use the term to mean the totality of three related but distinct capabilities that an individual can have:

1. *Intellectual capital* – the skills that people accumulate through formal and informal education and in the course of their work that can be translated into income through paid work.

2. *Social capital* – the family, friendship and other social networks
    and connections that provide people with access to potentially
    beneficial opportunities (for example, a personal recommen-
    dation for a job).
3. *Cultural capital* – the range of leisure and consumption activ-
    ities that one engages in and which help to differentiate one
    from others.

This analysis is very much built on the work of French sociologist Pierre Bourdieu (who in fact used the term *embodied capital*
for what we refer to as *human capital*). It is worth quoting Gershuny
– who is Director of the Institute for Social and Economic
Research at Essex University in England – at length to make this
clearer:

> We now (following the discussions in Bourdieu's *Distinction*[2]) think
> of societies as structured by the distribution of different sorts of
> embodied 'capital' . . .
>
> [This fits] better what we know of the 21st century, across much
> of the richest parts of the world.
>
> . . . we may now think, in a Bourdovian manner, of multiple sorts of
> resource which in different combinations give different levels and
> qualities of access to the various institutions – and hence the differ-
> ent sorts of experience – afforded by our societies. We have various
> skills in different sorts of consumption and organisational participa-
> tion – we play football, we organise social events for the synagogue
> or church or mosque, we cook food and give dinner parties, we listen
> to music. All of these activities give us different sorts of satisfaction,
> and different degrees of social status, depending on how fully and
> effectively we are able to participate in them. And in turn the effec-
> tiveness of these sorts of participation, and the extent of our engage-
> ment within the relevant institutions, depends in large part on the
> context, frequency and duration of our previous engagement in these
> activities. Our past experiences – or at least some of them (since others
> simply evaporate, and have no further significance) – progressively

congeal or cumulate to form personal resources, or capabilities. These congealed capabilities, all outcomes of our past time-budgets, are what Bourdieu called embodied capitals.[3]

The critical point about this argument is that employment (and the ensuing income) is only one element in the way people differentiate themselves and 'advance' in society. So, it is not just the skills, job and money that you have that are important but also who you know (to leverage that intellectual capital even more) and how the activities you do place you in some form of cultural space or hierarchy. This has been recognized for some time. As long ago as the early 1930s, sociologist Pitirim Sorokin was describing social mobility as being in two dimensions, while also linking it to the growth of individualism:

■ *Vertical mobility* represents the traditional concept of social class where there is an ordered hierarchy of social and economic advantage (that people may, or may not, move up or down in the course of their life)
■ *Horizontal mobility* is about how one differentiates oneself from others within any given allocation of economically salient resources.

Gershuny relates this horizontal mobility specifically to social and cultural capital – distinction and self-worth comes from whom you know and what you do in your non-work life as much as from a job or income itself[4]. Figure 4.1 illustrates this in diagrammatic form. The traditional employment and skills-based hierarchy (vertical axis) is now augmented with the two other dimensions. Apart from anything else, this explains why social class (which is based purely on occupation) is becoming a less useful predictor of consumer behaviour. It also begs the question as to why the marketing industry continues to rely on such a crude and incomplete classification system.

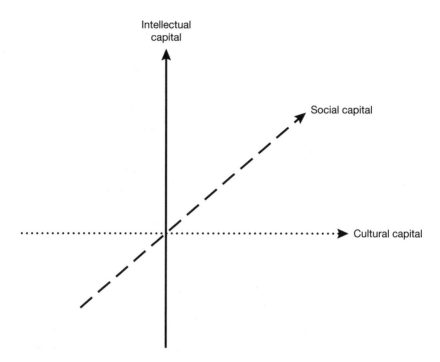

Figure 4.1   The growing importance of social and cultural capital. The three dimensions of human capital: differentiation increasingly derives from social and cultural capital as well as intellectual capital.

Source: based on Sorokin/Gershuny.

Some readers might wonder how this is relevant to our overall thesis of complicated lives. It is so because unlike material goods, human capital is less visible and more ambiguous; it is intangible and constantly needs replenishing. Hence, maintaining and nurturing intellectual, social and cultural capital – as we will discuss in more detail later – is a complex activity.

We have discussed in the previous chapter some aspects of social capital (and its growth in importance) so in this chapter we concentrate on intellectual and cultural capital. And to discuss intellectual capital we need to consider how the world of work is changing.

WORK AND INTELLECTUAL CAPITAL

There are many misconceptions about changes in the nature of paid work, not least that we spend more time at it than we ever did. This, as we show later in this book, is simply not true. And, although there is much debate about the end of a 'job-for-life' it is far from clear that there is much more 'turbulence' than in the past – academic studies have shown that average job tenure (the length of time spent in a specific place of work) has decreased by only a small amount over the last twenty odd years. But, that is not to say that changes have not occurred in the world of work and that some of these changes have made life more complex. For a start, there is certainly a perception that no-one can expect a job for life any more. (Whether, given increased longevity, anyone would want such a thing is another, and in fact highly important, question.) Also, evidence from Britain suggests that the process of establishing oneself in a career has become less stable for recent cohorts. Figure 4.2 shows that for young people today, the chances of leaving the first job have increased by some 13% per year, by

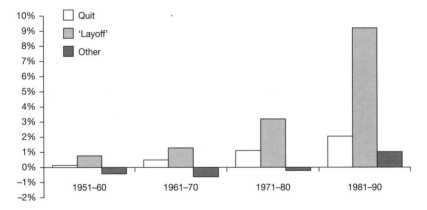

Figure 4.2 Increasing chances of leaving first jobs. Per cent chance of leaving first job within a year, relative to pre-1951 cohort, by birth cohort

Source: *Seven Years in the Lives of British Families*, Institute for Social and Economic Research[5].

comparison with people born before 1951. While this is largely due to increasing chances of being laid off, this also reflects increasing numbers of young people taking on short-term employment. In many cases this will be because this is all that is available, but it is also because first jobs are no longer so likely to be seen as an irrevocable career choice.

Whether or not there is, in fact, greater enforced job insecurity, there can be little doubt that there is a growing recognition of the importance of education and the intellectual capital that is gained from it. It is no surprise, therefore, that in Britain since 1971, the number of people enrolled in further and higher education has more than doubled, from 2.35 million to over 6 million today. The technology revolution (see Chapter 6) reinforces the importance of education and particularly knowledge management skills since in the digital world information and ideas travel much faster around the globe. This, and the change in the nature of work itself, means that more work can be done in the home or elsewhere out of the office. And, of course, you are contactable at all times and in all places. Thus, the routine of work has been demolished for many people. Again, this is not necessarily a bad thing – in principle workers have more flexibility (in, for instance, working around family care demands) – but it certainly adds another dimension to individuals' management of their days and the juggling of tasks that are required.

As the economy becomes more service oriented (see Figure 4.3) – and as a result there are more front-line, customer-focused workers – so all the talk from management gurus is of employee empowerment: the ability to make on-the-spot decisions to solve customer problems[6]. It is happening too in manufacturing where the move is away from the mindless (and unempowered) production lines epitomized by Henry Ford to the team-based units working together in whatever way is appropriate to meet the production schedules and quality levels that have been set. Although this is a welcome development, as jobs tend to be more

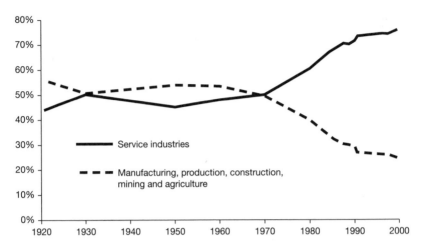

Figure 4.3 The fall of manufacturing and related employment. Proportion of the total British workforce employed in each sector.

Source: *The Rise of the Network Society*, Manuel Castells 1996/Labour Force Survey 2001/nVision.

rewarding, an inevitable result is that it makes the job intellectually more difficult. The growth of self-employment and of the cultural, creative and consulting industries[7] also means that there is more project-style work rather than continuous employment. This leads to what we refer to as the *hollywoodization* of work and a clearly less settled employment situation.

By this, we mean the way working practices are changing to reflect the growth in 'knowledge' work – which is by its very nature more project and contract based – and where, perhaps, Hollywood provides a model for what this actually means for those in such jobs. Consider the following aspects about life in Hollywood that could also, arguably, apply to the emerging workplace:

- It's who you know, as much as what you know.
- 'Talent' is the critical issue – judged on and rewarded accordingly.
- The need to constantly reinvent/reposition yourself.

- You're only as good as your last project.
- Image is as important as reality.
- Work is project related.
- Pay is project related.
- Fame is everything (and fame can be more important than content).

Charles Leadbeater made a similar point in his book *Living on Thin Air*:

> Imagine working in the film business, moving from film to film, crew to crew, set to set, a success one month and flop the next, a progress in which you are only as good as your last project. Work may be like that for many more of us in the next decade: at times fun and rewarding, but itinerant and punctuated by bouts of insecurity.[8]

This has implications for employers and employees alike. Employers will need to encourage, pamper and nurture their best talent as might occur with a fragile star in Hollywood. Employees will need increasingly to consider their own, personal employment brand. Intellectual capital will need to be constantly maintained; social capital (networking) will be critical.

Related to this is Richard Florida's concept of creative capital – the skills and capabilities held by those who are part of the *Creative Class*[9]. These people are 'knowledge workers, symbolic analysts and professional and technical workers' who add economic value through their creativity. It includes 'scientists and engineers, university professors, poets and novelists, artists, entertainers, actors, designers and architects, as well as thought leadership in modern society: non-fiction writers, editors, cultural figures, think-tank researchers, analysts and other opinion makers'[10]. Florida's analysis is both interesting and important as he shows that creative capital is key to the economic growth of an area and that such creative hotspots are diverse and tolerant.

So intellectual capital – and particularly creative capital – is more important, and managing and replenishing it is crucial. Economic growth areas will be more diverse. This all makes for a much more fun and dynamic society, but one with fewer 'givens', more change, more diversity and more complexity.

CULTURAL CAPITAL

This discussion of the knowledge and creative sectors leads inevitably to the growth of the cultural sector and the rising importance of cultural capital. This reflects not only the role of cultural capital as a means of differentiation and advantage but also the related, and growing, interest in experiences and fulfilment (Chapter 2). So, for example, American academic Jeremy Rifkin states that:

> We are making a long-term shift from industrial production to cultural production.[11]

And that:

> The meteoric rise of the entertainment economy bears witness to a generation in transition from accumulating things to accumulating experiences . . .[12]

As we noted earlier, the idea of cultural capital – in the sense that we are using it here – was first articulated by Pierre Bourdieu. According to him, status or distinctiveness (hence the title of his book *Distinction*) is achieved through the process of *leisure consumption*. Using their own personal capabilities (human and social capital) and, importantly, their financial resources, people establish a unique combination of leisure activities and competences that differentiate them in terms of a personal, distinctive lifestyle. 'Leisure, for Bourdieu, is a means for asserting individuality in a modern society'[13].

To a certain extent this has always happened. But, the point is that relative to material possessions ('accumulating things' as Rifkin puts it), cultural and leisure activities ('accumulating experiences') are now more important than they were. So conspicuous consumption (the possession of material goods) is augmented by less conspicuous consumption reflecting the gradual development of cultural capital and proliferation of consumer media. This takes social differentiation into a realm of less obvious signifiers. How, for example, does someone know that you are an expert in Japanese art or fine wines or paragliding? Only, of course, if they see you doing that activity or engage in conversation with you.

It is little surprise, therefore, that consumer spending on leisure, recreation and culture has grown over the last 50 years. Figure 4.4 shows spending on the category of recreation and culture for a range of European countries. Not only has it grown in real terms but it is a rising proportion of total consumer spending. In Britain, spending on services outstripped spending on goods for the first time in 1999 – having been half its size thirty years ago. Total

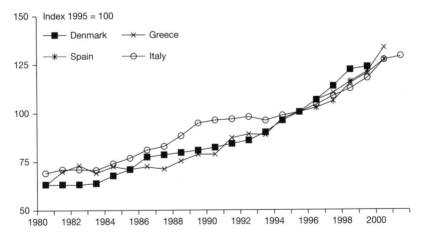

Figure 4.4 Spending on recreation and culture. Index (1995 = 100) of real spending on recreation and culture for selected EU states.

Source: Eurostat 2002/nVision.

spending on recreation and culture (which in this series does include some goods like audio-visual equipment) is taking a larger and larger share of consumer spending.

But, this clearly adds complexity to society. No longer are people categorizable purely by their visible possessions (important though these may be) – their interests and non-work activities are important too. (It is interesting to note that throughout history, the very rich have always sought to gain legitimacy and status by association with the artistic or cultural world. This remains the case whether it is celebrities getting involved in charitable work, sponsoring art or suddenly 'finding' classical music or opera. The important point is that this is now shifting down the income/ job-related hierarchies so that more people can distinguish them- selves as culturally different. This perhaps explains why more books than ever are being bought by the public even though the time spent reading them has not increased – bookshelves are full of unread titles[14].)

It is inevitably complex too because as the range of different leisure pursuits and their sub-categories grows (think of how the number of 'sports' that are included in the Olympics grows every four years), so the potential combinations grow too. A person can be a squash playing, bird-watching wine lover. Or be a ten-pin bowling, Greenpeace activist, Italian cuisine gastronome. And, as the classic, class barriers to many of these activities decline, so the potential mix increases (and hence the combinations and thus the prospective means of differentiation).

It is important to note that this is not necessarily just about 'high' culture (opera, classical music, Greek philosophy, great literary works) but embraces more popular culture too. In research we conducted for online news service Ananova we found that in Britain the great majority of people had a mix of high and low brow interests – in effect, a 'no-brow' outlook on life. In an increas- ingly democratic workplace and educational system, where people more often have to deal with people of different age and gender to themselves and with different backgrounds, the ability to fall back on the common experiences that mass culture can provide is increasingly valuable to all of us. This explains why the old boundaries between 'worthwhile' cultural topics and 'junk' are becoming blurred, and few people now wish to restrict themselves to extremely 'refined' interests. This is not to say that we are not interested in distinguishing ourselves by our interests, but that such distinction is not necessarily snobbish or hierarchical – it may equally well be about distinguishing ourselves as 'one of us' – especially for younger people.

So, an increasingly important component of our own identity is not only what we know (intellectual capital) and who we know (social capital) but what we are interested in (cultural capital). To quote Jeremy Rifkin again:

> In the new era, where cultural production is increasingly becoming the dominant form of economic activity, securing access to the many cultural resources and experiences that nurture one's psychological existence becomes just as important as holding on to property.[15]

THE THREE CAPITALS

In the modern world the skills and capabilities we have, which can be translated into monetary gain via work, are important – more so given the nature of the knowledge economy. Hence educational achievement becomes more vital. In a networked society, who you know (as Peter Drucker said – see Chapter 3) is as important as what you know, so your social networks are increasingly critical too. As affluence grows and financial barriers to many markets decline for the majority of people it is what you do – your interests and leisure pursuits – that define who you are as an individual. Your intellectual, social and cultural capital are all important. Its totality – your human capital – not only determines who you are, but how well you will get on.

This means that traditional ways of segmenting markets are less relevant (it is another way of describing fragmentation after all) but it does not mean that privilege no longer exists. In fact, it is helping to spur the polarization that we can see occurring in our societies. The reason is that the three forms of capital are not independent.

The main way this happens is through the influence of families. Thus, parents with high levels of human capital, coach and endow their children with cultural capital, manage education systems to maximize intellectual capital and use their contacts (their social capital) to promote their children's chances. Thus, one study in Britain noted that:

> The evidence . . . supports the idea that richer parents are likely to have a larger and more valuable stock of both social capital and intellectual capital to pass on to their children.[16]

Jonathan Gershuny has found that British middle-class parents are 'working' the education system 'to ensure high levels of educational attainment for their children'[17]. And it looks like the effect is getting more pronounced over time[18].

And our own research shows that those with higher educational qualifications are more likely to rate culture and knowledge as being important (Figure 4.5). They realize the cachet it has in the modern world of social hierarchies.

Here, then, we have one of the main reasons why the growing importance of human capital adds to the complications of life – it increases the concerns of, and pressures on, parents to help their children make the best of a less ordered, less predictable world. But, there is also the fact that in such a routeless society, where an individual is more dependent on their own generated (and family propagated) human capital and less on the certainties of the class they were born into, there is more work to be done to maintain status, position and identity. Skills need to be maintained,

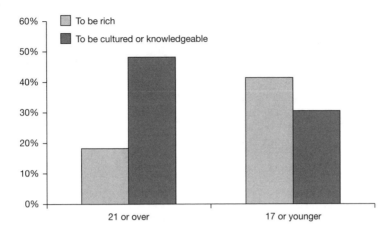

Figure 4.5 The ways people look for fulfilment. Proportion ranking each item first or second out of a list of seven aspects of personal fulfilment by age finished education.

Source: nVision, Future Foundation.

social networks lubricated, cultural expertise preserved. We have to work harder just to remain who we are.

As throughout this book, we make the point that this is not necessarily a bad thing (though some writers like Rifkin do take a pessimistic view of it) since people at least have the opportunity to change or reinvent themselves throughout their lives. But managing and reinvigorating human capital is, inevitably, more complex than was the case in the more defined and static world of the past.

The implications for business are clear. People will want more 'experiences' and to be able to define themselves by those experiences. They will want advice on how to start to build and then maintain expertise in certain activities (wine appreciation classes for example). There will be continuing opportunities for providing courses and training so people can add to the body of their intellectual capital. In all aspects of life – work or play – there will be opportunities in helping people nurture their human capital.

This will not be relevant to all product and service providers but for a surprisingly diverse range of suppliers it will be. Think of basic food products like an apple or a potato. Awareness of the varieties and different qualities, of recipes that can use the products, of what other foods (or drinks) they go well with are all potentially useful knowledge. Even in the humble potato there are associated elements of human capital.

CHAPTER 5

NEW LIFE COURSES, NEW CHALLENGES

How demographic change is affecting the way we view our life choices and opportunities

*I*mmediately after the Second World War, teenagers had a pretty clear view of how things would develop in terms of the stages of life they could look forward to. Life expectancy was around 65 in most countries, certainly not much more than official retirement ages. Most people got married (as they still do at some point) but very few got divorced. When they did marry, people tended to do so at quite young ages. Indeed in Britain from the immediate post-war period until the 1960s they did so at younger ages than at any point in history. Fertility rates (the number of children couples had) returned to pre-war rates. In the great majority of families, fathers worked and mothers stayed at home. As simple as that.

In such times, people's lives seemed to be clearly mapped out for them. Once they had finished school, men aspired to a job for life; for women, one that would take them up until they got married or had their first child. In terms of household arrangements, men and women expected, and were expected, to stay in their parents' home until they were married[1]. Having left to set up their own home, pregnancy would most likely follow soon after and the couple would settle down to a long period of nuclear family life – two parents with their dependent children at home. Somewhere in the long and distant future there might be a period of being alone as an elderly, retired couple. The same was true across the western world.

FROM SIMPLE TO COMPLEX LIFE PATHS

In the 1950s the post-war boom began. Affluence started to grow, consumer markets developed and people could have and raise children in a period of economic and social stability. Things must have seemed pretty certain and pretty good – with a clear path as to how things would be likely to develop. Although this certainty – and the certainty of how life might pan out – was not to everyone's liking (is it a coincidence that in the next decade, young people around the western world rebelled?) perhaps the stability of it all is why it is often imagined as a 'golden age'.

But how things have changed. Over that 50-year period, people are living anything from 10 to 20 years longer, representing about a 15% increase in life span in England, around 20% in France, Italy and Finland and a staggering 35% in Japan. Marriage rates are down, while divorce and remarriage is a relatively common event. Birth rates have plummeted in many countries with increasing numbers of women deciding to remain childless or, at the very least, to postpone the age of having their first child. People are leaving home to live alone and then coming back again. So, not only is life longer, but it has more stages, more choice and hence more complexity. What was a set, almost predetermined path in the 1950s is now a multiple set of paths and options – even demography has become complicated. As

Anthony Giddens has put it, we must 'become the authors of our own life story'[2].

To illustrate these points we take data from England and Wales, but the story is pretty much the same throughout the developed world. Figure 5.1 plots three different life events for women: birth of their first child; the age at which the last child reaches 18 (and therefore is deemed independent – even if, as we show later, many stay at home and semi-dependent well beyond this age); and death. All are average ages for women born at different times in history, with some guesses (and they are no more than that) from us on how this might develop in the future. Life expectancy is an estimate at age 20, as we are trying to look at women who had children and therefore want to exclude those who died young (of which, of course, there were many more in the past).

You can see that a woman born in 1850 and dying in the early part of the 20th century would have had precious little time, if any, when there were no children in her house. The vast majority of her healthy adult life was spent with, and looking after, children in her home. Contrast that with a woman born in 1950 and

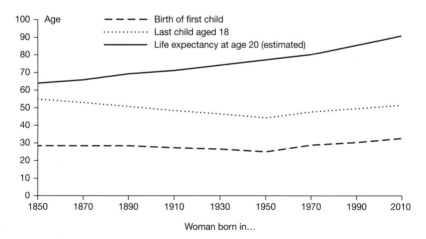

Figure 5.1 Changes to women's lives. Three life events for women born at different ages – England and Wales.

Source: Registrar General, *The Symmetrical Family*[3], Future Foundation.

whose last child would have been 18 in the 1990s. For her, most of her life is in the post family phase.

Thus the twin impacts of lower fertility and increased life expectancy are fundamentally changing people's life courses. On a population-wide level, one effect of this is that the proportion of nuclear family households has fallen dramatically over time and will continue to dwindle in the future (Figure 5.2). This does not herald the decline of the family, as such – most people still marry or have long-term partnerships, and most still have children – but rather that thanks to longer lives there are fewer family households at any given point in time.

But, it is not only that the relative size of different life-stages has altered but that there are more life-stages too. There is more variation in the age that young adults leave the family home and an increase in such people returning for a period at some point, there is a wider difference between women in the ages that they start to have children and there is the impact of divorce and remarriage. There are, as we said, more options, more choices.

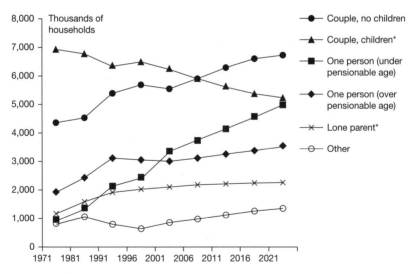

Figure 5.2 Household types, 1971–2021. England and Wales (* includes households with non-dependent children).

Source: National Statistics, Future Foundation.

It would be a caricature, but compared with the simple life plan of our post-war teenager who went from living at home, to leaving home and getting married and quickly having kids, to being retired, a modern day life might be something like this:

- Left home for university.
- Returned home after university.
- Left home again to live in a flat with friends.
- Moved into flat on own.
- Started long-term relationship.
- Co-habited with long-term partner.
- Had children.
- Got married.
- Separated and moved into flat on own.
- Moved in with a new partner.
- Child from previous marriage moved in.
- Part retired.
- All children finally moved out.
- Fully retired.

And, of course, there are multiple variations around these themes.

This increasingly diverse set of life courses and life options potentially makes things more difficult for an individual – it is not obvious what one should be doing at any given point in time, or what happens next. Don't get us wrong, there are clearly still relatively prescribed life courses involving education and work, partnership and children. But, as we have suggested, these can be less linear then they were (returning to education as an adult for example) or not as certain to happen at all (children for instance) or are less stable (partnership dissolution). More options mean less certainty; more choices mean greater complexity.

Recognizing this is important for business, not least in under-standing the personal complications that their employees might be facing. But perhaps the most important business implication is that stereotypical views of consumers and life-stage, of families and family relationships, are either out of date or irrelevant. This has important impacts on the segmenting of markets, since age – which has been probably the most used criterion in segmentation – is becoming a much less useful predictor of behaviour. And while it can be shown that life-stage is a much better classification to use[4], over time this is likely to become less relevant too (although the impact of having children will remain critical). Segmentation needs to be rethought around consumer attitudes and specific needs that will vary depending on circumstances at any given point in time. One way to do this is to consider the *transitions* that people make in their lives – from singledom to partnership, from non-parent to parent, from job to unemployed – and see how this affects their consumer needs. But before we consider that, we want to stay with family life, and particularly the impact of longevity upon it.

FROM SIMPLE TO COMPLEX (BUT ENDURING) FAMILIES

Apart from anything else, business and public service suppliers need to recognize that these demographic trends undermine the concept of a 'typical family', adding to the complexity of understanding different consumers' and families' needs. But this complexity and variation does not mean though that the family, as such, is in 'crisis' as numerous commentators have suggested.

For a start, there is not really any evidence of a decline in the importance of the central kin-relations of the nuclear family – parents, children and partners – in people's lives. The demographics of longevity, divorce and single-parenthood seem to give the decline of the importance of the nuclear family a kind of inevitability. But it is not that simple. We remain parents and children whether or not we live in a nuclear household, and most divorcees soon re-partner. As traditional institutions continue to decline in their influence over us (see Chapter 3) and fragmentation and individualism increase, the role of family ties as the psychological lynchpin of people's lives could actually be enhanced. As sociologist Manuel Castells has noted, for most people the family will be 'their rock in this swirling ocean of unknown flows and uncontrolled networks'[5].

Some research at the Future Foundation points to the enduring role of the family and those elements within the nuclear family in particular. This research[6] asked respondents in a survey to place various kinds of relation on a scale of one to seven, where one was 'no emotional attachment at all' and seven was 'a very close emotional attachment'. All the results shown in Figure 5.3 include only those who have the relative in question.

It is immediately clear that the idea of families in crisis needs qualifying – the nuclear family remains at the heart of most people's emotional attachments. Although longevity means a longer period spent outside the 'family' life-stage as such (and thus contributes to

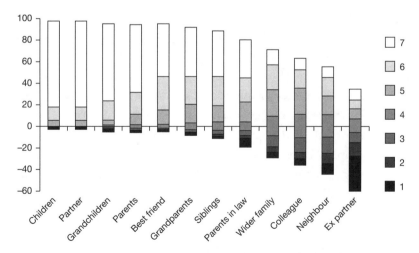

Figure 5.3 Closeness of attachment. Per cent giving each score, by type of relative/person – where 1 = no emotional attachment at all and 7 = a very close emotional attachment.

Source: nVision, Future Foundation.

the numerical decline of the family household) we do not detect any significant decline in emotional attachment to family among our armies of 'empty nesters' – those couples who are fit and middle-aged and whose children have left home. Our analysis shows that the vast majority of parents continue to give their children a score of 7 out of 7 even after they have left the family household. We can add this finding to the growing dependence of young adults on their parents (see Chapter 9) to make a strong case for the continuing importance of family life outside the family household, for both parents and children. But what happens when the next generation come along, and parents become grandparents? This is, after all, where demographic trends will impact on the vast majority of families, whereas the phenomena of relationship breakdown and multiple families still affect only a minority.

The question to consider, then, is not whether the family remains important – it clearly does – but more specifically the current status of the nuclear family. For, while in demographic decline in the sense that family households make up a smaller proportion of all households, it appears to be in emotional, sociological and ideological health – perhaps even ascendancy (remember our suggestion in Chapter 3 that it is becoming of growing importance in providing support and advice).

To tease out the consequences of this apparent paradox, that the family (in the sense of networks of relationships of care) becomes more important, at the same time as it becomes less important as a demographic category, we need to look beyond the household to the wider family. And, in particular, we need to consider the 'stretching' of the family across generations as life expectancy grows.

THE VERTICAL FAMILY

The structural changes that underpin the 'verticalization' of the modern family unit are clear. Improved nutrition and healthcare have led to greater longevity and more generations alive within a family; at the same time, falling birth rates produce smaller 'core' families and hence fewer siblings – and uncles, aunts and cousins. The result is an extended family that may be numerically of similar size but is increasingly vertical rather than horizontal in form[7].

Thus, grandparents are becoming an integral part of the modern family, and their role looks set to grow ever more important in the 21st century. This is where we come back to our earlier initial analysis on emotional ties to different family members. Readers will remember (Figure 5.3) that only one other relation comes close to the nuclear triad of parents, children and partners when it comes to attachments, and that is grandchildren. This reinforces a very important point about the nature of the vertical family: the lineages (blood ties) are more direct and it seems, therefore, that the relationships are deeper. In this way, the

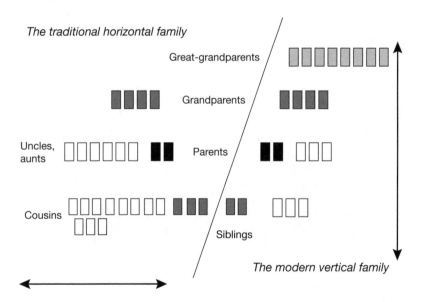

Figure 5.4   From the horizontal to the vertical family.

Source: Michael Young/Peter Willmott/Future Foundation.

potential influence of individual members of a family is greater, making family word-of-mouth recommendations and financial and other advice potentially more important.

There is, in all this, a happy story about life's complications: grandparents are working to alleviate them by helping with childcare. With more women working and greater concerns about the safety of their children (see Chapter 10), ensuring good quality reliable child-minding is a critical concern for parents. Fortunately, grandparents seem more than happy to help out.

Figure 5.5 suggests that there is a very striking trend towards increased involvement in childcare by grandparents as we move through the generations. The proportion of children who were ever looked after by grandparents was just one in three before the Second World War. This rises steadily through each decade, with 50% of children in the 1940s to 1950s having care from grandparents at some stage and around six out of ten in the 1960s to 1970s. The figure jumps higher during the 1970s, as more mothers returned earlier to work after having children, and in greater

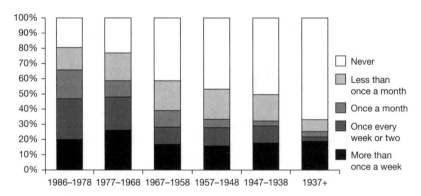

Figure 5.5 Grandparents and childcare. Proportion of people reporting whether/how often their grandparents cared for them when they were children, by birth cohort.

Source: *Complicated Lives Report*, Abbey National/Future Foundation.

numbers than ever. For children growing up in the 1980s to 1990s, four out of five had grandparents involved in caring for them. Much of this increase in grandparents' involvement is largely down to a grandparents doing regular, but relatively occasional childcare – that is between once a week and once a month. The proportion of children looked after by grandparents on this 'semi-regular' basis has leapt from just one in twenty to nearly 50% in the last two generations (since the 1940s/1950s).

Although, part of this result may reflect a degree of memory loss, with people forgetting the occasional babysitting of their grandparents as time passes, intuitively it seems a plausible outcome. As people remain healthy for longer there are simply more grandparents around to help out in this way. Also, we know that parents tend to go out more than they did in the past, requiring more help from those grandparents who are around. Certainly, analysis of time-use data over the years suggests that more time is being spent by people on the care of their grandchildren. Figure 5.6 illustrates the current extent of such help.

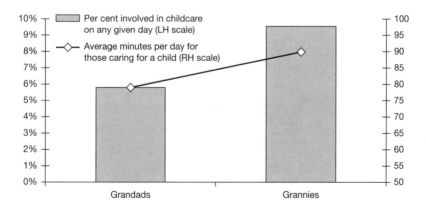

Figure 5.6 Childcare by grandparents. Proportion involved in childcare on any given day and amount of time spent doing so.

Source: National Statistics Time-Use Survey, 2000/Future Foundation.

THE TIME OF THEIR LIVES

But although it is clear that grandparents are responding to their children's need for help with childcare, we have to wonder whether the potential for involvement reaches a limit somewhere. The problem is that this generation of grandparents is wealthy, healthy and often focused on self-fulfilment – why should they want to add responsibility for childcare to their already busy lives? The fact is that these grandparents are having the time of their lives.

Figure 5.7 demonstrates that levels of satisfaction with life overall are actually lowest among those age groups most likely to be parents, namely the 30–50-year-olds – surely a reflection of the complexity and frustration of being a parent in the modern world. On the other hand, those aged 60–70, with the highest likelihood of being grandparents to young children, have overall satisfaction scores some 12% higher, and are, on this measure, the happiest people around today (alongside 15-year-olds, whose youthful optimism appears to be short-lived).

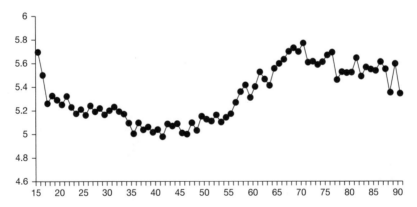

Figure 5.7 Satisfaction with life overall. Mean satisfaction score on a scale of 1 to 7, by single year age.

Source: British Household Panel Study, Institute for Social and Economic Research/Future Foundation.

We have spent some time discussing grandparents not just because of their importance in the developing vertical family (important though that is) but because the idea of a grandparent as a metaphor for the centre of gravity of modern societies is not a bad one. When thinking about the typical consumer over the coming decades the image of a grandparent – albeit a youngish-looking, healthy and reasonably affluent one – is probably as good a totem as you can get. Let us be clear here – we are not talking about a grey-haired, stooped and shuffling 80-year-old that regrettably, and mistakenly, is often the image that springs to mind. We are talking about the sixties generation (in which we include both those born immediately after the Second World War who were in their teens in the 1960s and those born during the 1950s and 1960s baby boom). The generation that is starting to approach grandparent-hood now.

Consider a woman born in England in 1950. She might have gone shopping in Carnaby Street in the late 1960s, had demonstrated against the Vietnam War in 1968 and seen Jimi Hendrix play at the Isle of Wight festival two years later. But, by 1975 – at the age of 25 – she could well have had her first daughter (the average age of first child for women born in 1950 was about 25). That child, on current trends, is likely to have her first child in 2005 or so (the current average age of first child is 30). Our swinging sixties rebel will be 55 years old and a grandparent.

Over the next 20 years in Britain the number of people aged 45–64 years will increase by 3.5 million. Across Europe the figure will be 20 million. This age cohort, as everyone knows, will be hugely important in consumer markets. Figure 5.8 illustrates the dramatic change in Britain over the next 20 years in the importance of different groups to shopping centre sales. Mirroring the point we made earlier about the changing numerical importance of middle-aged couples without dependent children versus family households, we can see that the so-called 'empty-nester' group will be the single most important one in shopping malls in coming

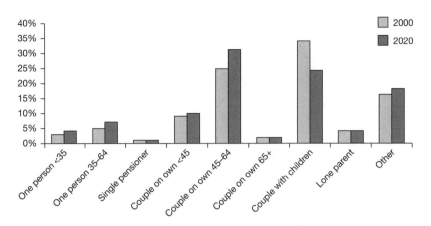

Figure 5.8 Shopping centre spending for different household types. Proportion of all spending at shopping centres accounted for by each group.

Source: *Shopping Centre Futures*, British Council of Shopping Centres/Grosvenor Estates/Future Foundation[8].

decades. So numerically but also financially, this age cohort will be critical for many businesses.

What an opportunity some readers might say. This is surely an interesting and potentially lucrative challenge for marketers? Unfortunately it is not as simple as that. For although those in this age group will spend on consumer goods they are quite a difficult and complex bunch.

First, as we noted in Chapter 2, as these people get older, they get more individualistic and harder to segment. They are also more demanding. Second, compared with previous generations (and presumably a function of the era they were brought up in) they are more likely to experiment and change their consumption patterns. In some research we have been involved in, we asked how often people changed various aspects of their lives. The stereotype of the older person is very much confirmed when you look at those aged 65 or over. The average person in this age group never significantly changes their hairstyle after the age of 41. And when it comes to clothing, styles were established even younger – the typical person of this age never completely changed the way they dress after the age of 36! Eating habits also seemed to be established by the time people got to 40 with the average age after which they never made a major change to their diet being just 38.

But Figure 5.9 shows how this stereotype will become increasingly invalid. Those aged 45–54 (and born in the immediate post-war period between 1948 and 1957, so including our fictional swinging sixties mother) are the *least* likely to have never completely changed their hairstyle or the way they dress. They even have lower ratings than those in the next age group down but this might be expected as they have lived longer and therefore had more opportunity to change. But this point also highlights the significant difference between the 'new' old and the current 'old' – the older groups have had more time to make such changes but many fewer of them have ever done so.

In the context of this book, the importance of all this is not that it makes life more complicated for people of this age themselves

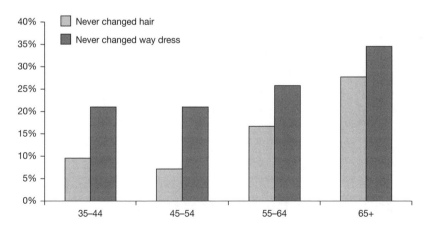

Figure 5.9 Sixties generation more open to change. 'When was the last time you completely changed the way you style your hair/the way you dress?' – proportion saying 'never'.

Source: nVision, Future Foundation.

except in the sense that they have a widening variety of options as already discussed. No, the big complication here is for marketers who seem to find it impossibly difficult to understand and target this group who are more diverse and more demanding. In contrast our research shows that it is young people who are more likely to 'follow the crowd', be influenced by advertising, to be more positive about brands and to rely on them more.

But, the bald finances of the ageing of the population mean that companies will have to devote more attention to this middle-aged group. The key question is why have they not already done so? We can think of two reasons.

The first is straightforward prejudice. In our experience, most marketers (we are thinking here of brand managers in their twenties and marketing directors in their thirties) do not see the 45 plus market as either important or sexy. Do we detect a bit of ageism here against those not of their own generation? This is, without doubt, one problem in some companies and with some individuals. But we wonder whether there is a simpler and actually less chauvinistic reason. We wonder whether marketers target the young because it is easier – they can be categorized more easily, are less critical; put simply they are less difficult.

This is not really the way to run business. And as the cultural and economic power continues to shift towards older groups, marketers will have to follow. There is a huge opportunity out there for companies that understand the needs of the baby-boomers who want to keep updating their lifestyles, and a huge danger for brands that fail to keep up.

UNDERSTANDING TRANSITIONS

To finish the discussion on changing demographics and new life-stages and life choices we return to the issue of transitions. One way to approach the increasing complexity of people's life course is to plot specific events at the same time as assessing their impact on any given activity, sentiment or market. This is important not least because there are more such *transitions* nowadays. Each generation moves house more often, and moves job more often (although the latter is only true of jobs *early on* in working life). Young people now take far longer to settle down into stable new family units, and there is the well-publicized increase in the likelihood of divorce and re-constitution of families.

If there is one statistic that sums up the cumulative impact of this on the lives of individuals, it would be this: a person born in 1930 could expect to get through about eight major transitions in her or his lifetime. The average person born a generation later, in 1960, has already made seven major transitions by age 40 (Figure 5.10), and might be on course for 12 in total. If it continued, this trend suggests that today's 16–24s might get through as many as 15 major life transitions.

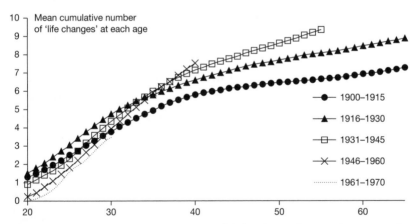

Figure 5.10 Cumulative number of 'life changes' at each age. Each line represents people born within the dates shown – events include getting married or divorced, moving into/out of cohabitation, house moves and job moves.

Source: British Household Panel Study, nVision/Future Foundation.

Our increasingly 'transitional' lives have huge implications for businesses, especially perhaps those marketing to the older consumer. The analysis shown above reveals not only increasing numbers of 'life changes' over a lifetime, but also, crucially, a shift in their pattern of distribution. In the early twenties, we see ever *fewer* life changes happening. But look at what happens after age 40 – where our oldest generation almost 'flat-lined' from 40 onwards, yet each successive generation is changing relatively more from that age. Perhaps this is unsurprising, as divorce rates in Britain have risen significantly faster among older age groups than younger ones in the last twenty years.

But – and this is the critical thing about looking at transitions rather than age, say – is that almost any event can happen to any person at any time. Who has more in common with a woman who has a baby at age 25: a childless woman of the same age or an older woman with a young baby too? Of course circumstances will vary, but new parents face common challenges, and we see fairly consistent effects on behaviour, attitudes and consumption patterns, regardless of age or social grade. While dads make a multitude of small adjustments to their time use (working more and contributing slightly more to domestic tasks, somewhat at the cost of their social life), mums have their lives turned upside down, massively reducing paid work and increasing unpaid labour[9]. We know too that having a child makes parents less satisfied with their financial situation and impacts negatively on savings behaviour. Financial strains are no doubt one reason why those in the child-rearing age groups tend to be less satisfied with life (as we showed earlier). Conversely, getting married makes people feel financially better off (the economies of scale of shared income). Again, while older people are generally happier, they are less so if they have just been divorced or separated, or lost a job. For people of the same age, there are huge differences in emotional state and financial situation depending on such life-changing events. Understanding these and marketing around them is surely the way forward.

So to conclude, there is a close link between 'life changes' and changes in consumption habits. Companies need to understand the implications of increasing social and consumer mobility not just on a general level but also in the sense that such life transitions may represent crucial moments at which to put a new offer to a potential customer. Moving in with a partner, having children, divorce, children leaving home . . . all these transitions represent points in life where needs, aspirations and disposable incomes can shift quite suddenly. And as they happen more often, they become more important for businesses to tap into. Companies need to examine their customer relationship management (CRM) strategies in this light. They also need to do all they can to get into, or create, the places and services that are associated with particular life changes.

CONCLUSION

So, we have seen that people's life courses are becoming more varied and less predictable; that families are in rude health but changing in form – from more horizontal to more vertical – with implications for family relationships and recommendations. We have seen how the ageing of the population is altering not only family and household structure but also the economic and cultural importance of different demographic groups within markets. We have discovered why marketers are frightened by this prospect and currently shirking the challenge. But we have also seen that the strength of the family is one counterbalance to life's complications (although as we discuss in Chapter 9, parenting itself can bring some specific complexities) and we have discovered that although segmentation will inevitably become more difficult, there are ways – by understanding and looking at *transitions* – that we can manage this better. Even demographics make life more complicated, not least for businesses still struggling with simplistic views and naïve stereotypes of what modern life really means for people.

CHAPTER 6

TECHNOLOGY AND COMPLEXITY

Why new advances make our lives more difficult while attempting to do the opposite

A ll too often, new technological advances are presented as solutions to an ever more busy and complex life. But the irony is that technology, while promising to make life easier, often does the exact opposite. There is little doubt that some of the greatest frustrations and stress-creators of the modern world are those appliances and applications that are meant to do just the opposite. How many of you have experienced the failed recording of a TV programme that was going to make life easier by time-shifting its viewing? How often has that word-processed document that is now in principle so much easier to store, edit and reprint been deleted, corrupted or lost in the black hole of a computer's inner workings? What do you do when the electric window of your car gets stuck open in a rainstorm?

Technology is not only frustrating when it does not work but it can also make things more complicated from the mere proliferation of devices in use in everyday life, the rapidity of their evolution and the complexity of their operation thanks to misguided, indeed myopic, design. But how bad is this effect? Has technology really made life so difficult?

LOVE AND HATE

In his book *The Rise of the Creative Class*, Richard Florida points out, quite correctly, that the technological innovations of the first half of the 20th century were considerably more dramatic than those of the years from 1950 to the present. However, we must not confuse great theoretical advances in the laboratory with technological advance in the average home. We cannot agree with his assertion that a time traveller from 1950 arriving in the present 'would know how, or quickly learn how, to operate most household appliances'[1]. Even those of us who have travelled here from 1950 the hard way have enough trouble – and it is not just the older consumer for whom the word 'programmable' can send a shiver down the spine.

Indeed, from the perspective of the consumer, 1950 is perhaps too long ago to begin our story. Only three decades ago the typical British home (which would have had a radio, a black and white television and a record player) would be installing a telephone for the first time. Domestic technologies were few, and more importantly, operated through simple interfaces – little more complex than an on/off switch and one or two other controls. Things that many people consider pretty basic today, central heating and a freezer, had yet to reach 50% of homes. Microwaves, videos and home computers did not exist as consumer products. Today, four-fifths of households have a microwave and a similar proportion have a DVD player or video recorder, although the latter is already becoming obsolete. Figure 6.1 would be unreadable if we included everything else which has arisen since then – answer-phones, mobile phones, DVD players, video cameras, digital cameras, personal digital

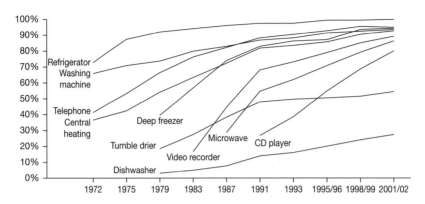

Figure 6.1 Technology take-up. Proportion of British households with selected durable goods, 1972–2002.

Source: General Household Survey/Family Expenditure Survey/Future Foundation.

assistants . . . in fact the list of high-tech consumer durables is more or less endless today. That is a lot of technology, and we have not mentioned the Internet and interactive television yet. On-line access is fast becoming the norm in British homes, with close to 50% of households on-line in early 2003[2]. The same is true across the developed world. Two-thirds of Americans have some sort of access to the Internet[3]. Around half of all European Union citizens have used the Internet in the last month, a figure that is forecast to go up to 80% over the next ten years[4].

Listing these technologies raises the question: if we are overwhelmed by the difficulties of coming to terms with such a proliferation, why would we keep buying them? Yet our research proves what we all probably see in day-to-day life – that consumers keep buying into new technologies, which many then struggle to operate on even the most basic level.

Consider, in this light, the data shown in Figure 6.2. Despite all the now discredited hype of the dot-com era consumers seem amazingly interested in a range of 'new' technologies. Such 'hypothetical' priorities should be treated with caution – after all, only

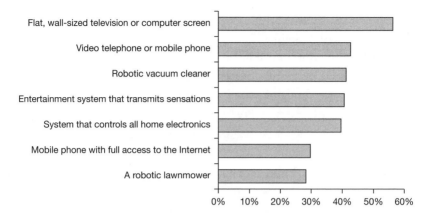

Figure 6.2 Interest in emerging technologies. Proportion of people who say that they would like to own each technology.

Source: nVision, Future Foundation.

one in ten people thought they would want a mobile phone at the beginning of the 1980s. But, with that in mind, the levels of interest we register in the various emerging communications, information, entertainment and labour-saving technologies we asked about are surprisingly high.

So, why are consumers such enthusiastic buyers of new technology?

Aside from purely aspirational desires (something we would not downplay, particularly among the small group of early adopter technophiles) this reflects a fundamental optimism and acceptance of the benefits of new technology. This applies at a general level and, at the moment, for modern communications technology in particular – as the high ratings for wall screens and video phones demonstrate. But note, there is already very significant enthusiasm for devices that could help with more mundane chores like the robotic vacuum cleaner and lawnmower (the rating for the lawnmower represents nearly half of those who actually have lawns).

This optimism in the ability of technology to bring about improvements in the world has been around for a while and shows no sign of abating. Future Foundation research shows that over 20 years ago in Britain 60% agreed with the statement that they 'welcome all technological advances for everyday living'. The same proportion feels that now[5]. In part, we suspect this relates to a recognition that basic fundamentals – like quality – can be improved by new scientific advances. A DVD player just delivers a better movie experience than a videocassette. The new technology *enhances* people's lives.

Yet, an equally important factor is likely to be a belief that it will also solve some of life's problems – it will *decomplicate* things. And this is the irony, because, as we have already noted, some technology turns out to be the bane of people's lives: making things more complex, not less so. There are at least four factors behind this:

1. The pace and breadth of change.
2. Techno-determinism, complication and feature overload.
3. More, and more complex, communications in the network society.
4. The blurring of the boundaries between work, home and play.

THE PACE AND BREADTH OF CHANGE

One of the reasons that people believe that technology is quickening the pace of life and making things more complex is because 'experts' tell them so. Writers like James Gleick[6] have warned of the effects of acceleration, complexity and unmanageable risk in modern life, while those like Neil Postman[7] see technology as often unnecessary, trying to solve 'problems' that don't exist, while often creating new ones.

But this is not a new theme. J. K. Galbraith was deeply concerned about the development and influence of the 'techno-structure', writing in 1968 'I am led to the conclusion that we are becoming servants in thought, as in action, of the machine that we have created to serve us'[8]. We can place Galbraith along-side thinkers from across the political spectrum, all of whom shared, to a lesser or greater extent, his concern about the role of technology in society – Martin Heidegger, Marshall McLuhan, Herbert Marcuse, Jacques Ellul (a particularly thorough-going critic) and Louis Mumford have all contributed to this debate.

A common concern is that technology gives greater weight to the values of efficiency, productivity, systematization and speed, over less easily measurable but no less valuable qualities of life. A good example of this is provided by Langdon Winner whose perspective on the development of 'speed-reading' techniques is worth quoting at some length here:

> . . . the combined emphasis upon speed and efficiency – increased words per minute plus increased comprehension – reduces an activity with many possible values to a pure instrumentality . . . The reader may now want to pause a minute to consider other instances in which things have become senselessly or inappropriately efficient, speedy, rationalized, measured, or technically refined. To ponder so will help make clear what is meant by the primacy of instrumental values. It will, however, cut your reading speed on this section considerably.[9]

This kind of criticism of technology, while less overt, continues three decades after its high water mark in the 1960s, and is clearly shared by many consumers – and with some justification. After all, technology does allow us to do more, to cram more into each unit of time, to seek information or speak to a friend immediately. We have seen acceleration in media content too, with cutting speeds in party political broadcasts, documentaries and advertising rising[10]. In part, this may result from the more competitive nature of today's media, but it is also a response to viewers' demands for more soundbites. It is not just that 'experts' are writing about a quickening of pace, people are really experiencing it. Thus technology for many is seen as inseparable from many of the organizational imperatives shaping the demands and pressures of the modern workplace, or more generally, the acceleration of everyday life.

But, it is not only the pace of change that causes concern but the sheer breadth of it too – there are so many more appliances and applications around. At one level, this just reflects growing affluence. Our own research among consumers[11] highlights a strong sense of a growing demand for consumer goods of all kinds, and particularly where children and young people are involved. Perhaps it is when confronted with 'pester power' that parents realize quite how strong the desire for 'new' technology can be. At one level, then, the proliferation of consumer electronics is associated with immoderate and frivolous desire, and the people we spoke to, even the younger ones, while positive about their own new acquisitions, often wanted to justify their purchase in terms of functional improvement and down-to-earth needs.

Probably the best metaphor for the electronic appliances and gadgets that overflow from people's homes is the remote handset. One of us has over a dozen controllers in his house, with five regularly on top of the main television: one each for the television, cable, DVD, video recorder and audio hi-fi. There is also a separate remote keyboard for interactive digital TV. Partly this represents the madness of duplication – why don't electronics suppliers make it easier to have one controller? – but it also just reflects the amazing quantity of devices in the average home. If you think this is bad, it is likely to get worse before it gets better (which it may well do as we discuss later). Just think what it will be like when robotics devices in the home become ubiquitous (as they will) or when remote controllers for lighting, heating, cooking and the like become the norm.

TECHNO-DETERMINISM, COMPLICATION AND FEATURE OVERLOAD

So more is happening, and – or so it seems to people – more quickly. But there is another problem with what might otherwise be potentially life-solving technology. It is not designed with the user in mind.

It is a sad fact of technology development and roll-out that it has been driven by the technology itself rather than the needs and demands of users – we have been prisoners of technological determinism. Technology has been put into the marketplace because it is there; because something new can be done that was not possible before, irrespective of any proven demand for the product or service. That is why so much technology fails – and why, incidentally, there have been some unforeseen successes like SMS text messaging. The massive and unexpected growth in SMS took place because there was a huge market for cheap, almost instant communication between young people (price was more important to them than synchronicity). Yet, no mobile operator fully anticipated this before they implemented the service. In our work with technology developers over the years we have been surprised how little notice they take of end-user needs. As one of the more enlightened ones said to us once: 'we have all this amazing technology we can put in the product but we just don't know what the consumer really wants'. Wrapped up in the technology, and the possibilities that it offers, the developers' views seem to be clouded – they focus on what can be done rather than what consumers might want to be done. It is no surprise that technology launches in the consumer arena are such a hit and miss affair. We fear that the same is happening now with the development and roll-out of third generation mobile phone products and services. And, if we could have one last gripe at technology companies, if they could make electronic products easier for the average person – who is not a techno-freak – to use that would help too.

We do not wish to be over-critical of designers per se – we have huge respect for what they do. Indeed, there is a growing emphasis on more user-centred research that takes better account of consumer views when assessing the prospects for new technology. Part of the problem is in companies (rather than the design industry) pushing innovation from an engineering or raw science perspective. As a recent conference in London noted:

> Products and services that have been inclusively designed are gradually appearing in the marketplace. Yet despite a strong commercial argument for adopting this strategy many companies are still wary of it.[12]

A related problem is that there is too much designed into products in the way of features and options. This is a difficult issue and an understandable problem for manufacturers since they are grappling with trying to match economies of scale with the increasingly fragmented needs of consumers that we outlined in Chapter 2. Their adopted solution is to build appliances that have more capabilities than most people need but satisfy the individual demands of the most ambitious user.

Readers will not be surprised to learn that many people own technologies with features and functions that they cannot actually exploit. In research we conducted for British bank Abbey National[13] we found a large proportion of people cannot make proper use of the gadgetry that they have in their homes. While roughly three in ten could not use all the features of their CD player, microwave or digital TV, this already dismaying proportion rose to almost half in the case of video cassette recorders, and was still higher in the case of Internet access (Figure 6.3). The interesting thing about the three in ten people who claimed they could use all the features of their home computer is that the great majority must be wrong about this, since this could only be true of a handful of IT professionals, if even them.

Although manufacturers might do better to reduce the specifications on some models, the temptation will always be to be more rather than less generous. This is understandable but means that this aspect of technology complication will continue for some time, until the features become smart and imbedded themselves – something we return to later.

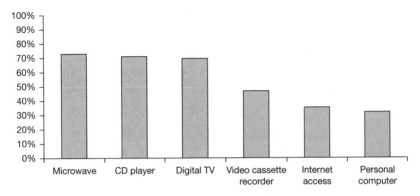

Figure 6.3 Too many features? Proportion of people who feel confident in using all features of each particular technology (excluding not applicable).

Source: Complicated Lives Report, Abbey National/Future Foundation.

MORE, AND MORE COMPLEX, COMMUNICATIONS IN THE NETWORK SOCIETY

One of the great consumer technology successes of recent years has been in communications devices. There is a reason for this. Humans are social animals and not only have a need, but actively want to communicate with others. As we have noted elsewhere in this book (see, for example, Chapter 3 – and, for that matter, Chapters 4 and 5), far from society, family and community disintegrating, they are as healthy, if somewhat changed, as they have ever been. And technology, rather than creating a more isolated, atomistic society, has helped in the growth of a richer, more connected world. The fantastic success of mobile phones – which allow us to communicate in places we could not before (irritating though that can be to those forced to listen in) – of SMS text messaging – which allows teenagers to do cheaply what they love: gossiping to friends – and most of all e-mail – which allows, fast, yet asynchronous, cheap, long-distance conversation – is ample proof of that.

Modern communications technologies are therefore an integral part of everyday life in the 21st century creating a virtual communications infrastructure that is inextricably intertwined with individual activity at home, work and at play. They are fundamental to the functioning of the 'network society'[14]. In the more fluid and flexible world in which we live, where individuals take increasing responsibility for the shape and meaning of their lives, technology plays an important, and largely positive, facilitating role.

But positive though this development is, it is not without its complications. For a start, the very nature and speed of these 'always-on' communications helps to create a perception of a faster pace, relating to the point we made earlier. There is a greater sense of immediacy in action and thought, fuelling a belief that the world is moving at an increased velocity.

Then, there is the flip side to increased contactability – those being able to reach you whom you do not want to. Our research has highlighted concerns about those situations where the individual was no longer in charge of the direction and frequency of communications[15]. Thus unwelcome contacts (usually in the form of marketing, by phone, e-mail, or 'pop-up window') and e-mail overload were widely raised in an on-line forum as issues[16]. A relatively new technology like the Internet, which many consumers do not feel fully in control of, is thus a particularly bad environment for uninvited offers.

And then there is the sheer variety of different channels we can use. We all need to manage and orchestrate a variety of communications methods across the growing virtual infrastructure to get what we want out of life. Each person has to be responsible for learning to use the various technologies to maximum effect, knowing which are the most appropriate channels to use and when. Say you have a complaint against a company – do you go to the shop you bought the goods from, telephone the manufacturer or visit its website? The more communication options we have, the more choices we have to make and that, as we show in the next chapter, is an added, and not always welcome, task in life.

So, the explosion of communication technologies is positively welcomed by consumers (why else would they be so successful?) because these technologies enrich people's lives as social beings and give them more control over time and space. Yet, it is not without its costs. It increases the perception of a 'runaway world', as Anthony Giddens has labelled it[17], it opens us up to unwanted incoming messages and it creates an ever greater, and ever more complex, range of channels to use and abuse.

THE BLURRING OF THE BOUNDARIES BETWEEN WORK, HOME AND PLAY

The final element of complexity that technology introduces is in its ability to break down the boundaries between different aspects of people's lives. This is something that is happening anyway as a result of the declining influence of society's institutions on life choices, behaviours and routines and the changing nature of work that we have discussed in earlier chapters. But technology certainly is assisting this trend. In particular it is affecting the relationship between work and home and where and how we 'play' (and what constitutes play).

Mobile communication devices and the Internet are two of the main developments assisting the blurring of the lines between different environments and locations. For example, 15% of respondents in a British survey use their home Internet connection for work purposes and similarly around 17% of workers are accessing personal content via work connections[18]. This 'blurring' provides a powerful demonstration of the way in which emerging technologies can facilitate a whole new way of interacting and communicating with key networks from different geographic locations. And it seems that these connections are not driven by the technology itself, but by the social, professional and family needs of users.

New technology does not only break down the association between particular places and activities. What is less often noticed is the way that it is blurring and redefining categories of activity themselves. For example, we are already witnessing the gradual disappearance of the boundary between 'gaming' and other kinds of activity. There is a physical element to this as the majority of new games consoles now include some form of physical feedback through control pads or joysticks, and we are beginning to see more advanced interfaces simulating driving, golf, dancing or shooting, for example. We have also recently seen the development of various ways of integrating exercise machines with games consoles, and the growing concern with health and fitness makes these sure-fire winners, as well as having the potential to evolve into systems for detailed personal health monitoring. It is not only the electronic gaming versus exercise distinction (which has been much worried over by commentators on child obesity) that is set to disappear – we should also consider the distinction between electronic gaming and fiction, performance, learning, media consumption, artistic endeavour, personal relationships, even pet-care . . . All of these and more have increasingly become integrated with technology-mediated 'gaming' (is this term even appropriate any longer?). The 'ludic' potentials of digital technology should be on the agenda of companies who, at first glance, have little to do with gaming. There may be more spheres of activity to which gaming elements can be brought than might be imagined. We cannot see any limit, in principle, to the ways in which companies might interact with their customers, or provide currencies and contexts for interaction or game-play. As Wacker and Means point out:

> The tendency to merge work and leisure – and to make each moment of both do double duty – is not confined to the work-

place or work-related activity. We play when we work at the everyday stuff of life, too, and we do so just as fervently and out of just as great a necessity.[19]

The physical boundaries between technology and user are also becoming harder to draw. The next decade will see platforms for broader physical interactivity move rapidly into homes in the form of games, learning, interactive exercise and sports practice, and possibly more personal interactions – recent years have seen dramatic increases in the sales and social acceptability of electronic hardware here. Although some commentators have discussed the 'disappearance' of technology, as processing units become hidden, leaving only free-standing wireless interfaces (for example screens or keyboards), it is the *appearance* of technology in new places and forms that consumers will be more interested in. More everyday objects that are, or even double as, interfaces with the digital world will emerge while the evolution of 'direct input' mechanisms like gloves, headsets and pads will bring new devices altogether into the home. As 'technology' invades more and more objects, places and activities, its association with any particular type of object (as in the PC 'box in the corner') becomes harder to sustain. Of course, a lack of clear-cut distinctions between places, activities, times, technologies, people and things is not necessarily a bad thing in itself, but it is likely to make life a lot more complicated.

LOOKING AHEAD

Looking forward, what can we learn from this review of technology innovation and its implementation into everyday life?

At this moment in history, it is easy to be sceptical about new technology and its impact on human lives: its capability to enrich and enhance human existence. But, the billions of dollars, pounds and every other currency wasted on the dot-com boom (including the huge amounts spent on third generation mobile licences) clearly reflects the enduring power of technology hype and techno-determinism; and continuing failure to appreciate consumer needs and demands.

This is why consumers tend to fail to live up to the expectations of technologists, and in their turn, are rarely entirely happy with new technologies. There is a chronic need in technology companies to look first at their customers. To be fair to companies, this is particularly difficult since consumers are not very good at anticipating or articulating how new technology might help them in their lives (and certainly not when one is discussing some hypothetical point in the future). Part of the problem is that traditional market research is not so good at testing potential consumer take-up of new technology and a recognition of this is a reason why we get the technological determinism that we do. But there are techniques that go beyond standard market research that can identify underlying needs and opportunity areas. An understanding of what really matters in consumers' lives and how that is changing and the 'pressure points' that arise can provide major insight. So too can psychologists and industrial designers versed in the mediation between technology and people.

Important in this is the very fact that technologies adapt or are appropriated by consumers to suit relevant and emerging needs. So, the evolution of human needs and technological capabilities continue to drive each other on, as they always have. But the result, and this is a rather important point, is that those who win out will be not those who understand technology as such but those who appreciate and exploit technofusion – the integration of technology into consumers' lives, and vice versa.

So what areas of technology development might do well in the future? It is not our aim here to consider this in detail, since our concern is the role of technology in alleviating or not life's complications. But there are two areas in which, in this context, we can foresee good prospects.

The first is further labour-saving devices in the home, where robotics is likely to have an impact as prices fall rapidly (Figure 6.4): lawnmowers and vacuum cleaners being two examples that we highlighted earlier. This builds upon the consumer's historical enthusiasm for labour-saving devices, particularly where the perceived value of the labour in question is low (for example, most types of housework). The fact that the time spent on housework has not fallen as much as it might have is because much of the potential time saved by labour-saving technologies has been eaten up by rising standards of hygiene and cleanliness. The idea that today's younger generations constitute a 'dirty generation', as some commentators on falling time spent cleaning have portrayed them, is in fact false for this reason. And, it does not indicate that there is any diminution of interest in time-saving devices in the home.

Thus, rising standards of cleanliness, together with an ageing population and ever-increasing pressure on housework time, create the likely prospect of the continued proliferation of robotic and

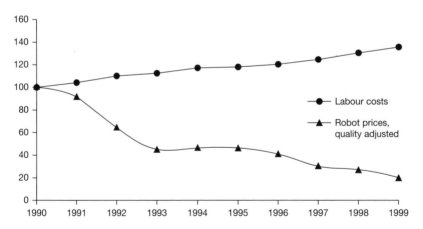

Figure 6.4 Cheaper robots. Robot versus labour costs (United States) – Price index: 1990 = 100.

Source: UN Economic Commission for Europe/International Federation of Robotics.

mechanical assistants in the home. This is turn will fuel the need for integrated, user-friendly control systems for domestic technologies, which again, sizeable proportions of people already express the wish to own. Generally speaking, the more complex and 'intelligent' our home systems become, the more crucial it will be to address issues of control and usability – the example of video recorders (where, if we recall, over half the British population cannot understand all its features) cannot be allowed to occur again.

The second area offering good prospects for technology that helps to decomplicate our lives is in the area of communications. We expect continued growth in mobile technologies, with Figure 6.5 suggesting as many as 90% of European citizens owning a mobile phone by 2005. In some countries, notably Scandinavia, Italy and Britain, it could be even higher and compares, in Britain, with a figure of only 3% in 1988. The mobile phone may also be an example of another important development which we pointed to in Chapters 2 and 4. Whereas in the past people often

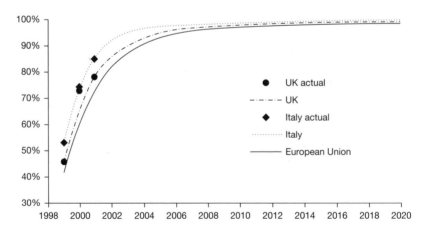

Figure 6.5 Mobile telephony in Europe. Proportion of adults owning a mobile phone – actual and forecast. European Union as a whole and selected countries.

Source: Eurobarometer, nVision Europe.

desired objects explicitly because the product would enhance other people's perception of them, there has now been a subtle shift to people wanting such items because they will enhance their 'quality of life'. Mobile phones in the 1980s were something of a yuppie lifestyle statement, whereas now they are sold as a useful tool that can transform your work or social life. Going forward, we anticipate mobile devices being used by consumers to help manage, control and, in some instances, simplify things.

But, this brings us back full circle to the question of whether technology does indeed make life more complicated or less. In the past, and despite its benefits in many areas, mobile telephony has also, at the same time, made the pace of life seem faster, has added a new media channel (adding to channel proliferation) and has been over-featured, making it difficult to use for some. To date, technology has in many ways made life more complicated.

Unlike Neil Postman – who admits that he has a reputation for it – we are not anti-technology. But we do agree with a critical part of Postman's analysis: that somewhere in the 19th and 20th centuries we became obsessed with innovation for innovation's sake. As Postman puts it, 'the great invention of the nineteenth century [was] the invention of invention'[20]. And in the last twenty or thirty years, he points out, we seem to have forgotten to ask the question 'what is the problem to which this technology is the solution?' We have got to the point, as Postman notes, where 'there are technologies that are employed – indeed, invented – that no normal person would regard as significant'.

If technology is to stop complicating our lives and start making them easier, then the design and implementation of it must become more user-centred. Its proponents must be able to answer the question of 'what problem does it solve?' That is the challenge for the future.

CHAPTER 7

THE CHOICE EXPLOSION

*C*onsumer choice is not only one of the fundamental principles of modern western societies, it is also one of the starkest differences between these countries and less advantaged ones. The supermarket in communist Russia selling only thousands of pairs of size eight work boots, the relentlessly basic diet of most of the world's population; these throw into sharp relief the cornucopia of consumables, heaped eight feet high down endless thousands of miles of shelving, that is available to those in advanced economies. It is a good bet that the majority of our readers are well aware of an increase in the number and specificity of products in the markets they are usually concerned with, and many of you might consider this an entirely benign, and consumer-led, phenomenon. Yet consumer choice becomes an urgent issue when we see it in totality. The scale and complexity of choice is the subject of an exponential growth that has taken consumers into a new landscape, unrecognizable a generation ago, where choices stretch beyond the horizon, dwarfing our ability to survey and select.

How has this happened? In part, it reflects a growing consumer demand for choice as affluence grows and individualism flourishes. But there is also a supply side push to this – the outcome of globalization, flexible manufacturing processes and deregulation has been more open, responsive and competitive markets. The suggestion here is that the reduction in trade barriers allows companies to enter new markets, bringing new choices to consumers and encouraging competition and innovation.

Some argue that we are not witnessing an increase in choice at all, since standardized global products 'crowd' out local ones. But it has to be remembered that many such local players were operating in conditions that were, in effect, local monopolies. Although there have clearly – and sadly – been local casualties, it is harder to prove that choice has been reduced. So, setting aside any judgement about whether this is a good development or not, think about those French and Italian consumers who can now enjoy a McDonald's burger – something they could not do before 1979 and 1985 respectively. And clearly, given the success of the company in these and other countries there is a real demand for the product.

DROWNING IN CHOICE?

This points to an interesting development: an increase in choice within markets, while at the same time a decrease across markets. The two should not be confused and there is, therefore, a perfectly legitimate argument that those companies that are accused of commoditizing the world have, in fact, at a global level helped to drive a more diverse set of tastes and offers. We recognize that for many people this will seem a contentious view. So often people complain about the pernicious spread of McDonald's, Coca-Cola, the Gap, Walmart and other multinationals across the globe. (It is not a coincidence that such complaints are normally directed at American companies.) But this is as much a reflection of a concern about a decreasing variation across markets (the reduction in local diversity) as an objective measure of the choice available to a shopper in a local supermarket in any given country. It may be a 'bad' development, but it is one only really affecting the middle-class, cosmopolitan, international jet-setter constituency.

And, as we showed in our orange juice example in Chapter 1, consumers can be offered a significant range of choice (in this case over 20 varieties of juice) from a few brands (in this case three). The same is true of soft drinks where Coca-Cola, Pepsi and Cadbury Schweppes can provide a dizzying array of options. (Coca-Cola alone has more than 300 beverages in its portfolio.)

But, this does present problems to those very same global companies. As more and more consumers become individualistic and cosmopolitan so they demand yet more choice and differentiation. So, despite their success over the last 20 years, this is the challenge the likes of McDonald's and Coca-Cola face not only around the world in markets they have entered fairly recently but in their home markets too, where newer, fresher, more individualized and more sophisticated competitors are challenging their positions.

So, the increase in choice also represents companies' attempts to try to meet the consumer demand for it. As affluence rises, discretionary income increases and consumers become more confident in their own individual choices (as we noted in Chapter 2), so tastes fragment. There are fewer economic, social and institutional constraints to what people can and cannot do; fewer peer group or value-based barriers to choice. No one could argue that the choice explosion has happened in the face of consumers' opposition to product differentiation, or that choice is inherently bad. But these largely positive driving forces have given rise to an unforeseen problem. There is a good chance that the ideal product for an individual's needs is out there in the marketplace, but how can they find their way to it?

The consumer's freedom to choose has long been a central strut in liberal political philosophy. But, and this is the crux of the problem, enthusiasm for choice has always been predicated on the consumer's ability to find the best deal in the marketplace. This is what Adam Smith assumed when he said that competition:

> can never hurt either the consumer, or the producer . . . Some of them, perhaps, may sometimes decoy a weak customer to buy what he has no occasion for. This evil, however, is of too little importance to deserve the publick attention, nor would it necessarily be prevented by restricting their numbers.[1]

Those politicians who have embraced the market economy and proclaimed that the expansion of consumer choice was central to their mission reflected the same enthusiasm. But neither Smith, nor perhaps the politicians, can have foreseen a world in which markets have become so multiplicitous and so complex that the activity of choice itself might cost the consumer more than any value they might derive from the process of comparison. Time and information are now essential elements of any analysis of modern consumption, and consumers and regulators alike are developing responses to over-complicated markets. Businesses too are responding, but innovation is limited, and there is a growing danger, in an infinitesimally fragmented marketplace, that the efforts of marketers will disappear into white noise.

As we look at the increase in consumer choice in more detail, there is a further dimension to bear in mind. Consumers can now draw upon a dizzying range of considerations, as ethical, ecological and health issues are brought to bear upon product choices. Is this product safe? How was it produced, and who by? And of course, these questions complicate a more fundamental one – what does buying this say about me? Signifiers of social status and personal identity are more complex and nuanced (as we discussed in earlier chapters) – and now almost universally considered in everyday consumption.

When Jean Paul Sartre said 'obviously I do not mean that whenever I choose between a millefeuille and a chocolate éclair

I choose in anguish', he perhaps did not anticipate the kinds of significance that consumer choice can now take[2].

Today's consumers are subjected to exhortations from marketers, the media, academia and pressure groups that have vastly increased in volume and visibility. These interventions, alongside burgeoning wealth, have replaced the simple mathematics of affordability with the complex semiotics of self-representation and the angst of responsibility.

So consumers, at an aggregate level, want more choice and producers are – on the whole – able to offer it. Yet this provokes complication for two reasons.

First, although at a market level there may be a demand for greater choice (and a growing one as tastes fragment), at an individual level there may not be: some people are just not interested in some markets. For any given product or service – cars, hi-fi, holidays or life insurance – there will be people who want more choice and those who want less. Let us take a hypothetical example to make our point. Consider consumers in the 1950s. Most people would have been interested in the same markets and had a choice between, say, two or three brands. Choice was manageable whether or not you were interested in the market. Nowadays, not only have the fragmentation of tastes and the development of new markets and sub-markets meant that there is more differentiation across markets, but there are more choices within it too (remember the Tropicana and Coke examples). Choice is manageable in those markets you are expert in and completely bewildering in those that you are not. The result is that for many consumers in many markets an excess of choice is, indeed, a burden.

Second, even where people might want choice, they do not have the mechanisms and information to negotiate the available options open to them.

THE CHOICE EXPLOSION

Shopping gone mad?

In many cases, the rate of increase in consumer choice has been nothing less than explosive. The most obvious place to look is the high street. In grocery retailing, the local grocer has given way to the supermarket, and supermarkets have grown into hypermarkets, in some cases stocking more than 70,000 product lines. This growth has occurred in less than a generation. For example, at leading British grocer, Tesco, the average number of lines per store has grown from a mere 5,000 in 1983 to over 40,000 today. Bookshops have followed a similar pattern, and are now stocking as many as 200,000 titles. A visit to an American supermarket discovered over 50 different marinades/barbecue sauces from 15 different brands. Even stopping to get a cup of coffee may present us with more choices than we would like to confront. Our local coffee bar offers 11 types of coffee, 4 added toppings, 3 types each of milk and sugar, 3 sizes of cup, and the options of decaffeinated and/or extra cream. In all, that allows for over 6,000 different permutations of a cup of coffee!

The proliferation of competing products across so many product areas reflects an ever-greater elaboration. Take cleaning products. Whereas the Victorian housewife or maid knew twenty different applications for vinegar as a cleaning product, the average home now has more than six different household cleaning products. We see ever smaller functional or aesthetic niches being filled, as separate products have emerged for use on floors, windows, bathrooms, toilets, kitchens, ovens, in the form of creams, mousses, wipes and sprays, available in a range of scents and finishes and with various anti-bacterial properties. But this is a very generalized phenomenon – we also see increasing diversity in basic foods, with economy, standard and premium variants now being joined by organic, low fat, nutrient-enriched and otherwise health-enhancing variations.

Children now have basic foods re-produced and re-packaged for their individual tastes. (Tropicana, as we noted in an earlier chapter, has a special 'Healthy Kids Orange Juice'.) Of course, the proliferation of choice on the high street has not happened in a vacuum. Our lifestyles and expectations have altered as dramatically as the range of goods on offer to us.

Routine consumption, where the same meals or activities would always happen on the same day or at the same time, is disappearing. In Britain, spending on meals bought away from home has risen from 11% of food expenditure in 1968 to around 25% today[3]. A far greater range of food is eaten, increasingly often encompassing the traditional dishes of other cultures, or indeed inventing them, as in the case of tikka masala and ciabatta bread. London's restaurants now offer the cuisine of over 150 different nations and regions.

Clothing exhibits an even more dramatic trend in terms of the 'domestication' of product choice. Where underwear is concerned, we know that the quantity purchased each year has risen to five times the amount bought in the 1950s[4].

Even boring things are complicated

Home ownership and foreign holidaymaking have become part of the lives of increasing numbers of people of the past two generations, and these bring a range of new choices into consumers' lives. But perhaps more striking still is the emergence of a multitude of choices in markets where recently there was none at all. One example is the impact that privatization has had on utilities markets across the world. We will use Britain as an example, but the same is true wherever markets have been created in previously publicly owned areas like energy and telecommunications. Just 20 years ago in Britain's utility markets there was effectively no consumer choice for gas, electricity or telecommunications.

Research for British energy provider nPower[5] identified a choice for the average consumer of 16 electricity suppliers, 22 gas suppliers and 7 telecoms suppliers (we include here the mobile service providers, and the minimum number of fixed-line suppliers available to UK consumers)[6]. Independently selecting suppliers for each service would mean a total of nearly *two and a half thousand possible utilities solutions*. And this is, of course, only at the level of the supplier. Each supplier has multiple tariffs, incentives and offers that make price comparisons extremely difficult and of only very temporary validity. Indeed, a source inside the industry has suggested that some offers are deliberately designed to prevent easy comparison. The mobile phone market also exhibits this complexification of pricing. While the number of companies offering services doubled, the number of different payment tariffs on offer multiplied twenty-fold since 1996[7].

Have consumers kept up? The average person thinks that they can choose between 12 gas and electricity suppliers in the UK, underestimating the number of competitors in the market by more than half – the true figure was actually 28 different suppliers at the time of an Ofgem study[8]. Consumers have remained completely unaware of many of their supposed 'options'. Perhaps more importantly, respondents were also asked what they would consider an *ideal* number of suppliers to choose between. The average here was just six to seven suppliers. Where the utilities are concerned (and we think this finding has a much broader significance), it appears that consumers only want to confront about a *quarter* of the choices that are actually out there.

This said, more than 40% of energy customers have switched supplier since deregulation – so there is movement – but does this really reflect an *active engagement* with choice? Only a half of switchers had made their *own* comparison of prices – the rest had to take on trust the promotional material of their new supplier. A mere 5% had consulted *Which?* (the independent consumer advice magazine), 4% had been to a website that compares prices, and only 1% had obtained a factsheet from Ofgem (the energy regulator). Around a quarter said they had 'seen pricing information in the media'. Clearly, utilities consumers rarely use up-to-date and genuinely impartial advice.

This brings us to the issue of the sources of information that consumers draw on – surely, with all this choice, there must be more advice to exploit too? Indeed there is – and then some.

An explosion of media output

Just 20 years ago, the average British consumer could choose between three channels on television. Today, there are around a hundred times this many channels. Even the free-to-air offer provides consumers with a selection of some 14 channels. A similar proliferation has happened in the number of radio stations, while newspapers have fattened with supplements, many of them orientated to consumption advice. Our study of trends in the production of national news for Ananova[9] provides a graphic illustration of the explosion of media output in the past couple of decades.

Let us imagine that, in 1980, there lived a woman who was obsessed with knowing what was happening in the world. She assiduously reads every word of every national newspaper, listens to every scrap of news on national radio stations and watches every minute of news broadcast on television. She may only sleep half an hour a night, and spend every remaining minute of her days consuming news, but she can just about stay abreast of the national news.

Today, our budding omniscient would struggle. It will take her two and a half weeks of continuous watching, reading and listening to consume every bit of national news produced in a day. Alas, while she does this, almost 7,300 hours worth of news will have been produced, which will take our red-eyed media hog the next 10 months to get through, if she can stay awake that long. By the time someone tells her that these days you can get news on the Internet and your mobile phone, too[10], we must hope that she is safely in the care of more selective information gatherers.

If this explosion of news production seems striking, bear in mind that the growth in public affairs material in the media has been far outstripped by the growth in non-public affairs material, encompassing sport, entertainment and 'advertorial' content. Consider also the explanation for this shift of emphasis in the mainstream news, the massive growth of the 'consumer magazine' sector since the 1970s, and we can see that media choices, and within these, potential sources of consumer information, have proliferated as much as any market in recent times. The information market only seems to heap more competing products into the equation.

HOW IS TODAY'S CONSUMER HANDLING CHOICE?

Understanding consumer decision-making

Clearly, then, today's consumer stands in a more ambiguous relationship to choice than those of twenty years ago. While the expansion of choice certainly reflects more powerful consumers in the sense of *spending* power, we should not equate this with the power to choose. Consumers certainly don't *feel* 'all powerful'. The issue businesses must focus on is where and when 'choice overload' is occurring in the experience of consumers and how consumers' choice processes are evolving in response.

We have to accept that these days, there are few markets in which a reasonable person would do what is necessary to make 'optimal' consumption choices. As rational choice theorist Jon Elster points out in *Solomonic Judgements*[11], making optimally rational choices requires not only access to options, but also the necessary time and information to choose, too. Spending too much time gathering information on a relatively insignificant choice is a form of irrational 'hyper-rationality', yet for many years choice theorists in the field of economics constructed models that ignored these critical dimensions. Where we see 'sub-optimal' choices being made, is it consumers who are inadequate, or our understanding of their motivations?

Interpreting the limitations of consumers' choice processes as irrationality is the easy option, and rarely yields useful insights. Considering them 'apathetic' (as many political commentators do) is still less sensitive to real life. No, we are not data-crunching calculating machines, and consumer competence is not evenly distributed between people or situations, yet we are never ultimately unreasonable decision-makers. If consumers handle impossibly demanding choice situations with selective attention and preconceived choice strategies, it is precisely because they are reasonable, and have better things to spend time on than the minutiae of product information and the mathematics of value.

Managing choice: how consumers cope

Our research reveals a range of different 'short-cuts' that consumers employ to deal with choice. Trusted brands obviously play a very important role here, and they will continue to do so. Before we return to this though, some interesting alternative approaches to managing choice emerged as well. It seems that the more choices we have to make, the more inventive we have to be to manage them all.

The majority of our respondents spontaneously mentioned various ways in which they 'self-limited' the choices on offer to them. Routine re-purchasing was the most obvious way of doing this, alongside the 'ostrich' approach to markets where choice is relatively new – consumers simply ignore it altogether. Some used broadly based value judgements: one always bought organic food because she believed in it but also because it made choice easier; another said that his habit of only buying reduced items was as much about not having to think about what to buy as it was about price savings. Similarly, one respondent plumped for an ethical investment package because that guaranteed some 'value' to the investment without having to confront the difficulty of finding the optimal investment solution.

Clearly then, consumers often make their choices by avoiding consideration of other options altogether. Obviously, one response for suppliers is to identify and target such niche markets, tapping into the particular concerns that characterize particular sub-sets of consumers. But there are other, and more interesting responses to the complexity of consumer choice.

WHAT COMPANIES CAN DO

What is the moral of this tale? When, in even the most apparently suitable of markets, consumers largely fail to embrace their choices in a proactive way, should we not simply accept that the winners will be the companies who out-market the competition? Or do we attempt to limit consumer choice – to wind back the clock a couple of decades?

We think both these responses are potentially fatal to business. We need to accept that with increasing affluence, the desire for individualization and the trend to globalization, an absurd proliferation of choice is probably here to stay. So attempting to deny or limit consumers' choices, relying on myopia, inertia and pushy marketing will be increasingly less effective. It is those who genuinely help consumers to access or manage choice more effectively that will prosper. Over the next decade, we predict that choice management brands and retailers can do well, retailers and service providers who make use of technology to empower consumers will benefit, and that in many sectors sustained best-value offers will become harder to compete against. Consumer empowerment remains an unrealized opportunity.

Yet there seems to be a culture within some companies that finds the reality of consumer empowerment hard to come to terms with. In financial services, the tiny minority of consumers who do vigilantly move their funds to obtain the best returns are labelled 'rate-whores' or 'rate-hogs' – one almost gets the sense that getting the best deal out of companies is some kind of cheating, the practice of a tiny 'rogue element' in the marketplace. Companies need to respond more positively than this. Consumers and regulators[12], aided by technology, are going to evolve responses to the choice explosion, partly with the help of businesses who realize that they can gain competitive advantage by genuinely helping their customers.

Getting the right approach to choice management

Big price or product differentials obviously make engaging with choice in a market a higher priority, and by extension make the choice management function of services, retailers or brands that much more valuable. But the *way* in which consumers will want to engage with market choices also depends very much on how their individual interests and experience relate to the particular product and the particularities of the purchasing situation. There are at least six factors that affect the consumer's approach to choice:

1. Interest and knowledge in the category.
2. Previous experience and confidence in the market.
3. Whether there is enjoyment of the process or experience of choosing – this will clearly relate to the qualities of the retail environment.

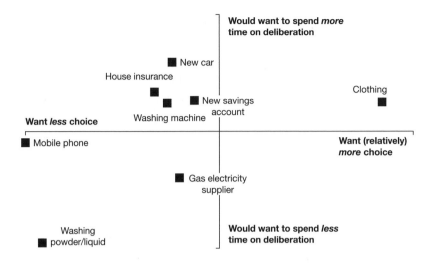

Figure 7.1   Wanting more time is not the same as wanting more choice. Markets plotted on whether people feel they should spend more time on choosing (vertical axis) by whether they feel they need more choice in the market (horizontal axis – see Figure 7.2)

Source: nVision, Future Foundation.

4. The amount of time they can, or want to, devote to the purchasing process (see Figure 7.1). As James Gleick points out, enjoyment of a situation is strongly related to perception of time[13], and of course it is *perceived duration* that really matters. This is to say that speedy service and consumer enjoyment, or the lack of them, will multiply the effect of one another.
5. The perceived *risk* of engaging in choice at all.
6. The perceived differential between products or services in a sector. Significant differentials in *price savings* or *functionality* will make choice management more attractive.

Our research gives clues as to how these trade-offs affect the level of enthusiasm for choice in various markets.

In an area like energy, where consumer choice is a relatively recent and perhaps not enthralling prospect, there is less enthusiasm for personally confronting a wide range of choice, despite the existence of fairly substantial price differentials. The perceived *risk* of engaging in choice where a multitude of alternative choices have unstable pricing (for example interest rates or utility rates) or unknown quality is also a key factor in the utilities and financial services markets. This is where genuinely trusted brands acting as proxy for the consumer, or as editors of choice, will attract customers. The average saving that would persuade a person to switch utility supplier is no less than £78[14]. If this figure is any measure of the value of the perceived risks, time and effort required to engage with choosing a new supplier, then it is also some measure of the potential value of the market for choice management services.

In other areas, such as clothes, where many consumers invest identity and leisure time in developing knowledge in the product area, and where many people gain real pleasure from the purchasing process, people will respond to the challenge of choice in a different way. Such consumers may not want choice taken out of their hands at all, turning to those agencies or retailers who facilitate active decision-making most effectively. Big *symbolic* differentials between products mean choice management has to play a relatively more facilitating role, partly by creating, managing and distributing useful or enjoyable information, and by being closely attuned to individual preference.

The importance of helping consumers manage choice is graphically illustrated in Figure 7.2. In all the markets concerned, few people felt they needed more choice. The implication is clear. What people need are not more options, as such, but better and easier ways of choosing.

Two broadly different, but by no means exclusive, responses to choice management have emerged from these considerations: we can call them *facilitating* consumer choice; and *representing* consumer choice (taking it off their hands). Our readers can hopefully decide which opportunities apply to which of their markets and customers.

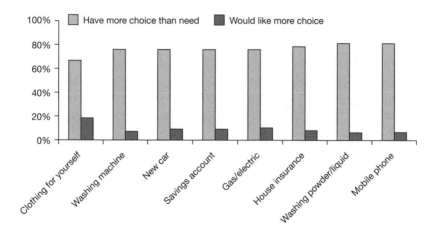

Figure 7.2   Few people say they want more choice. In a question, people were asked to score their attributes to choice in various markets, where 1 = 'there are currently more choices than I need' and 7 = 'there is not enough choice'. The figure shows the percent of people saying they have more choice than they need (score 1–3) and those saying they want more choice (score 5–7).

Source: nVision, Future Foundation.

Facilitating active choice management

By facilitating active choice management we mean providing readily accessible, relevant and comparable information about products to consumers. This will appeal when time cost is low, or interest high, where product differentials (especially symbolic ones) are seen as significant.

At the same time as choosing becomes more complex, the consumer's ability to interpret and pass on information is growing. Rising levels of education and diminishing illiteracy and innumeracy rates have produced a population where almost everyone has the basic competences of consumerism, and more analytical, reflexive and critical modes of thinking are becoming increasingly common.

The explosion of media content and channels undoubtedly means that more information is available, yet at present consumers, who are largely dependent on broadly 'advertorial' content for consumer information, rarely actively manage it. However, technological developments could have a huge impact in this area. The key difference the Internet makes is not in information production (there is plenty in any case), but in information access and still more importantly information management by individuals. And by 2010, it has been forecast that 90% of people in Britain will have Internet access through PC, TV or a mobile device[15].

Why then has so little use been made of such comparative services to date? Our research[16] reveals that there is a very strong relation between experience of the Internet and participation in particular types of online activity. It is only after two to three years of online experience that the percentage engaging in consumer activity (aside from simple 'window shopping') really begins to climb, and that proportion is still rising among people online for five years or more. At present only a very small proportion of the population has enough familiarity with the Internet to really engage with consumer information management, but a fairly rapid growth in their numbers should be expected imminently. It is still very early days in the technical evolution of Internet-based consumer support services and it would be extremely unwise to think that such scarcity of use is any indicator for the future.

In the near future, online retailers who effectively harness the information managing power of the technology by enabling customers to 'filter' products against any or all of a range of criteria (for example, price, performance, brand, ethical status, dietary restrictions) will give many consumers a power that the high street will never be able to supply. Looking somewhat further ahead, the development of shopping software and intelligent agents are intriguing prospects that could increase exponentially consumers' ability to manage their own choices.

Choice management and choice management brands

It is also likely that consumers will want to have their choice edited or chosen for them by third parties. In this sense, trusted brands will be in a strong position to have consumers' choices 'delegated' to them in this way, and we expect ongoing diversification of the range of products that are offered under the banner of the big brand names who get it right.

Generally, where perceived differentials are low or non-existent, a choice management service or function will not command much value, but consumers may be more inclined to delegate choice to a trusted (or merely familiar) brand for that very reason. This applies to both retailer and manufacturer brands.

The role of the retailer will continue to shift where global trading reaches direct to the doorsteps of consumers. The connoisseur could theoretically choose between an almost infinite range of products in many sectors. The concept of broad choice in a supermarket or other outlet becomes less salient in such a world. Instead of professing to maximize choice as many still do, retailers and the brands they sell may position themselves more explicitly as trusted editors of choice in a world where choice is limitless. Are we taking our orange juice example too far when we point out that in this Floridian supermarket there is a market leading international brand, a local one and retailer one? The choice provided in terms of trust and recognition (leading brand), familiarity and loyalty (local brand) and value for money (retailer brand) might be a model for many other markets. Choice is there – but it is managed.

But the role of choice manager for the consumer is not an easy one to master, and becomes more difficult in proportion to the extent that choice is being actively managed by the company. We believe that enduring consumer cynicism and persistent regulatory pressure will go hand in hand with technology-mediated information management to ensure that choice managers, be they retailers, manufacturers or service providers, who fail to represent genuinely the interests of their customers will come under increasing pressure. However, those choice managers who consistently deliver on their promise are likely to go from strength to strength. Certain markets can be overcrowded with brands who differentiate their image more clearly than their product and who over-claim on their 'personality' and its significance to the consumer. A brand explicitly positioned as a 'choice management' brand should simplify, not increase, the amount of baggage that it brings with it. Its primary function is a mark of trust rather than a mark of the consumer's identity. This takes us on, finally, to the ways in which companies can 'assure' consumer choice.

In some markets – where the difference between offers is in principle easily quantifiable, for example financial services and utilities – there is certainly a growing opportunity for companies who promise to provide consumers with the best value offer that is sustainable in the long term, or who promise to match the best available offer on the market. Of course, some retailers have been successfully trading on a similar promise for many years, but such offers can now be applied to other markets.

Where this is the case, independent sources of evaluation who can offer confirmation will provide increasingly valuable support. Furthermore, where consumers have confidence in the value of the offer, word-of-mouth recommendation can be an extremely powerful force, especially as it is increasingly possible for personal communications to be integrated with commercial or independent sources of information.

Doubtless these ideas are merely the tip of the iceberg when it comes to helping consumers manage choice, and this is an area where serious strategic thinking will be called for. But the problem of consumer choice is now so vast, and the politics of choice management changing so rapidly, that companies may be made or broken by their response to these issues.

CHAPTER 8

REGENDERING LIFE

*T*hat modern life is less subject to the constraints of traditional gender roles is hardly a startling revelation. Yet beyond this truism there are important questions which business needs clear answers to. Does the gender revolution still have momentum and if so where will it be taking us in the next twenty years? What are the actual consequences for men and women's lifestyles and consumption habits? As one commentator has put it[1], the 'newest type' is 'a hermaphroditic parental composite, the working man/woman in the grey flannel suit, the 50s mom and the 50s dad, everyone's beloved emotional refuge at home, a polished, well compensated pro, exuding confidence and bonhomie at work, a real nurturer without whom the mortgage would not be met.' A daunting prospect indeed! And one that has created some difficulties for commentators on gender, too: if we are indeed entering an 'age of androgyny'[2], what use will gender be as a tool for understanding anybody? Many seem to be using gender only to proclaim its demise.

One could imagine that the gender revolution has already dissipated into countless individual solutions, where both men and women freely share life's tasks according to individual preference or circumstance. At best, this is premature by about half a century. How men and women handle their changing relationships is still the subject of a complex compromise between inherited expectations and new economic realities. To illustrate the processes and negotiations involved in this area, in this chapter we focus on three aspects of the gender relations: work, everyday tasks and finances.

EDUCATIONAL PERFORMANCE AND EARNINGS POWER

The starting point in any discussion about gender must be the economic progress of women – its current momentum and future trajectory. To do this, we look at Britain, where as recently as 1970, before the introduction of the Equal Pay Act, working women earned an average 63% of the hourly rate that men did. The figure has risen significantly since then, to 81% today, pushed on by better-qualified women, moving into better-paid sectors, and attaining more senior positions (Figure 8.1). Women aged 16–34 now earn an average wage worth more than 95% of their male counterparts. If current trends were to continue, women would be earning the same hourly rate within a generation.

And there is little suggestion from recent trends in Britain that women's progress towards a greater economic role is slowing[3]. Many of us might be surprised to see that in many ways the gender revolution has continued apace in the last ten years. Although progress in the equalization of hourly wages has not been as strong in the last decade as in those preceding it, at the same time women have continued to move into employment. Women's ascendance to more senior positions in the workplace is another factor. Although the very top end of the management hierarchy is still overwhelmingly

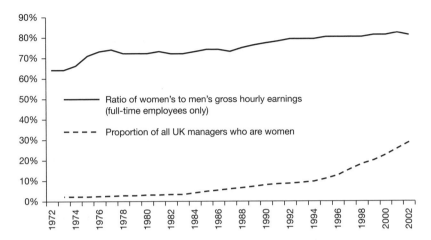

Figure 8.1 Women's earnings relative to men's and level of seniority in the workplace.

Source: National Statistics/National Management Salary Survey/nVision.

male-dominated, the 'glass ceiling' has been comprehensively shattered for management positions in general. One of us recently gave a presentation to the marketing department of an international drinks company and found the whole group to be women (apart from the marketing director of course). In Britain, the proportion of managers who are women was a mere 8% (less than 1 in 12) in 1990 – that has surged to over a quarter today[4].

Furthermore, British women overtook men at every level of education during the 1990s. In 1990, women accounted for only 46% of undergraduates but by 1993, female undergraduates outnumbered male for the first time, and in 2000, there were more women than men at postgraduate level too (having accounted for only 41% of postgraduates in 1990). Meanwhile, the gap at undergraduate level has swelled to some 183,000 extra female students, or five female undergraduates for every four males. Across the European Union as a whole, the predominance of women in further and higher education is equally pronounced. Trends in education, aligned with continued elimination of physical, unskilled and non-social jobs from the labour market, provide the most compelling reasons to expect ongoing economic progress for the women of the 21st century, and further role changes that would accompany it.

WOMEN ON TOP?

So does this herald an eventual *reversal* of gender roles? A European perspective cautions us against naïve extrapolations from current trends. Over the 1990s, the rate of male and female employment has converged in 13 countries of the EU 15. But in Sweden and Finland, where the female employment rate was at around 95% of that among men a decade ago, female employment rates have actually fallen back slightly since the early 1990s.

It is also crucial to consider women's job *tenure*. The proportion of women employed part-time varies dramatically across Europe and is generally associated with a high overall rate of female employment. In the case of Sweden, where the overall rate of female employment is almost identical to that among men, shorter working hours mean women are still contributing only 45% of overall national working hours (and this is easily the highest rate in the EU). The Scandinavian example is a sobering reminder. Despite having the most advanced legislative structures for female economic empowerment, it appears that progress here has stalled – and parenting roles have a big part to play in this.

Up to the present, motherhood has stymied the career progression of many women, causing women's wages to peak around ten years earlier than men's, while men continue to increase the value of their work and their total earnings. What evidence is there that younger couples will *want to* pursue more equal career paths, or even role-reversal?

In some research we conducted, a 40-year-old woman provided an example of the widespread *hypothetical* acceptance of the notion of the female breadwinner. She told us:

Nowadays you could get a woman solicitor marrying a lorry driver and so it makes sense for him to stop work and become a house-husband.[5]

Having said this, we should note that this particular hypothetical marriage is statistically about as likely as winning the lottery. Even where less extreme cases are concerned, it is still quite unusual for women to out-earn men in partnerships. Women in Britain are now earning more than their partner in 11% of partnerships, and incomes are roughly equal for a further 18% of couples[6]. However, the majority of these instances are among childless couples – parenthood tends to reassert 'traditional' roles in couple's lives[7], whether through full-time motherhood or the effects of temporary withdrawal from the workplace or part-time work upon women's career trajectories and earnings.

That is one reason to doubt that such role-reversals will rapidly become very much more common. We can also look at agreement with two statements, 'I prefer/would prefer to be the main breadwinner in my household' and conversely 'I would be happy to stay at home if my partner earned more than me'[8]. Unsurprisingly, younger women are significantly more likely to reject the role of housewife, yet a slight majority still say they would be happy to stay at home if their partner earned more. Even more starkly, only one in four say that they would prefer the role of breadwinner. Perhaps this merely reflects young women's hopes for their partner's earnings, but it hardly suggests a generation that is poised to take up the economic reins. On the other hand, an astonishing six out of ten men say they would be happy to accept the prospect of playing the role of househusband if their partner was the chief income earner – but whether, in reality, men would accept the burden of unpaid labour and the degree of economic dependence quite as happily as they would like to think is another question.

Whatever the actual outcome on this question, it is clear that a growing majority of mothers, and a gradually increasing number of fathers, will have to make pragmatic, complex, and arguably more rewarding compromises between earning and caring roles.

HOUSEWORK AND SHOPPING

As women work longer and increase their bargaining power, men have been called upon to increase their involvement in domestic labour. The increase in men living on their own also influences the equation. Time spent by British men on domestic tasks has increased by 99 minutes per day since 1961. This makes for an increase of some ten and a half hours a week on average.

Apparently, though, women are not doing less 'domestic' activity overall. Despite labour-saving devices, we have seen a four minute a day increase between 1961 and 1995. But note that women's activity has shifted away from cooking and housework and towards childcare and shopping. Much of this increase may be in 'leisure shopping'. The line between domestic labour and leisure is difficult to draw, but we can be certain that the trends point to a definite equalization of domestic labour, that is to say, working status rather than gender will determine it. On current trends, full-time women and (all) men in Britain will spend the same amount of time on cooking and housework as early as 2015 (Figure 8.2).

Another implication of greater equality in the home is that we may see women having to give up their traditional domination of domestic space in favour of a more negotiated, or even divided arrangement. Bedrooms and living rooms cease to be the exclusive domain and expression of female tastes as men's space moves in from the shed, attic and garage. There is, inevitably, more negotiation.

Have routine shopping chores followed the same pattern though? While they have clearly become more evenly distributed between men and women as time has gone by, the process of equalization is slow.

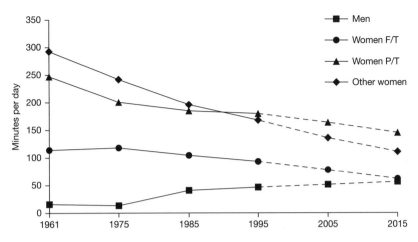

Figure 8.2 Housework forecast, by gender and working status. Minutes per day spent on cooking and housework, 1961–2015.

Source: *Complicated Lives Report*, Abbey National/Future Foundation.

Assuming an equal tendency for biased responses on the part of men and women[9], Figure 8.3 suggests that women are doing most of the grocery shopping in roughly half of partnerships and men do most in about 1 in 10 partnerships. The remaining 40% (not shown in the figure) share it equally between them. This rate of change suggests that it might be fully 80 years before women can expect men to be taking an equal share of grocery shopping.

This said, we forecast that increasing equalization of working hours, and the ongoing shift to 24-hour retailing and Internet shopping, will mean that the majority of couples will share grocery shopping equally by around 2020.

This is one example of the way that changing gender roles suggest important new segmentations – these 'shopping sharer' couples will have particular approaches to shopping, and understanding the way that they negotiate shopping tasks will become a key issue for consumer goods manufacturers and retailers. Gender does not cease to exist as a driving force of social change, it is just that it used to intersect much more closely with other major

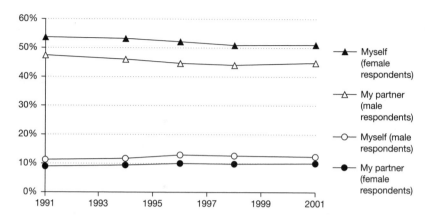

Figure 8.3 Main responsibility for grocery shopping, by gender 1991–2001. Proportion of respondents claiming main responsibility for grocery shopping lies with themselves or partner (chart excludes those who report 'shared' responsibility).

Source: British Household Panel Study/Future Foundation 2002.

determinants of lifestyle, particularly working status and spending power. So one could 'smuggle in' all sorts of convenient assumptions under the heading of gender segmentation. Increasingly, segmentations that directly use gender have to be more fine-grained, especially where women are concerned. For, as researchers from Warwick University's Institute for Employment research have pointed out, as women become more equal to men they become *less* equal to each other[10]. But in a world where labour is shared rather than divided, the real opportunities may lie in understanding the needs of men and women in their *relationships to one another*.

GENDER AND FINANCE

When it comes to day-to-day spending, however, there is a further dynamic to take into account. Greater equality is interwoven with the increasing financial independence of today's couples. Even without the influence of cohabitation, greater chance of divorce, and a more individualistic, less role-bound culture, the scope for individual freedom with money would have increased hugely over time, as increasing affluence has widened the scope for discretionary spending in general.

A 40-year-old man in our research gave us a compelling picture of how tightly controlled family finances sometimes needed to be in the 1950s:

> My mother used to put my Dad's suit in to the pawn shop on a Monday morning, you got paid on Friday so you get the suit out, have a good weekend and then take the suit back on Monday to get the money for the week. My old man he knew nothing about it – in and out every week.[11]

For many housewives at this time, day-to-day 'independent spending' was not so much suppressed by attitudes, as by the fact that domestic economies tended to make men the sole possessors of what were often, by today's standards, minute sums of disposable income.

The 'right' to spend independently is increasingly recognized among successive generations as Figure 8.4 shows. Despite this, independent spending is not a 'once and for all' arrangement. Many couples enjoy a period of relative affluence during their late twenties, when a couple's income is often greater than its expenditure. But, children bring relative financial strife (and initially at least, economic dependence for many mothers) until the late forties. Then there is a period of income/expenditure surplus through to retirement. As couples move from one stage of life to the next, independent spending will become easier or more difficult at various times in life.

So, this is yet another area of complication in life that relates to the nature of changing life courses discussed in previous chapters. With gender relations changing over time, financial roles may have to be renegotiated several times in a couple's life. Independent spending, though it is generally a positive development that is welcomed by most people, is by no means unproblematic.

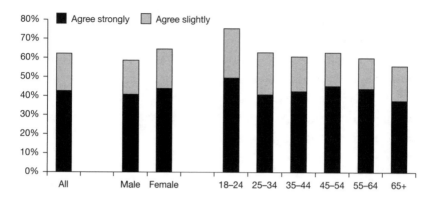

Figure 8.4 Agreement with the principle of independent spending. Proportion agreeing with the statement 'Aside from joint expenses, everyone has the right to spend their own money on whatever they want without asking their partner first'.

Source: *Complicated Lives Report*, Abbey National/Future Foundation.

TO BUY OR NOT TO BUY

Buying things without prior agreement still causes the most arguments between couples, with one in four married or cohabiting people saying they sometimes argue because of this. One way or another, money is seen as the prime cause of conflict by nearly one in five couples[12]. Other research has suggested that money disputes are a common factor in divorces.

Younger couples are far more prone to arguments over money than older ones, especially where contributions to household expenses are concerned. Part of the reason must be that it takes time for couples to establish a stable understanding of their financial relationship with each other. Perhaps arguments are one way in which couples negotiate the difficult issues that money can raise, and fortunately, it seems most couples eventually reach a mutually agreeable financial modus operandi. However, as life courses become more volatile (see Chapter 5), this makes it harder to establish stable understandings between couples. Financial roles will be renegotiated more often.

We think companies could be doing more to help. One obvious idea would be for financial service providers to help couples to set up a system of accounts – with, for example, debit cards for the joint account and credit cards on the sole accounts – that reflect a balance between independence and interdependence. The statement from the joint account could also outline who is spending what. The promise of 'no more arguments' would clearly appeal to those key young couples.

WHO PAYS?

It is clear that men have historically tended to take over on major financial decisions, and have often had some leeway in the proportion of their wage that goes to the family in the first place. Controlling money in this sense is thus a different ball-game from managing day-to-day expenditure.

To approach this issue, we separated 'day-to-day financial decisions (for example, paying bills)' from 'major financial decisions (like choosing a mortgage)' in our research. This distinction reveals that control of the big decisions tends to remain with men, and control of 'day-to-day' organization of finances is more likely to be the female partner's role. Overall, men make most of the major decisions in a quarter of couples, whereas women dominate big decisions in only one in six[13]. When it comes to the more trivial, regular, financial decisions, women do most in four out of ten of couples, and men do most in a quarter[14]. Here too though, we are seeing a changing division of financial roles emerging.

Interestingly, as Figure 8.5 illustrates, we see that men's domination of the major decisions is accounted for by the big discrepancy among *older* generations, especially those aged 55 and over,

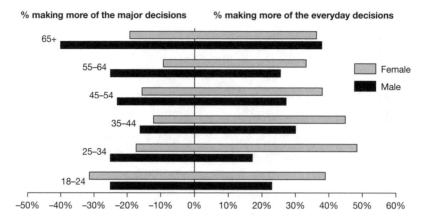

% making more of the major decisions   % making more of the everyday decisions

Figure 8.5   Who makes financial decisions? Proportion of men/women who claim to make more of the major financial decisions in the household, and proportion of each claiming to make more of the everyday financial decisions. (Base: couples only; chart excludes those sharing decisions.)

Source: *Complicated Lives Report*, Abbey National/Future Foundation.

whereas female responsibility for day-to-day financial decisions is largely due to those in *younger* age groups.

Between 1991 and 2002, the proportion of couples in which men had the final say in financial decisions fell from 25% to 20%[15]. This was mainly fuelled by an increase in the proportion of couples who claimed they had an equal say, from 65% to 68%, whilst the proportion in which the female partner had the final say rose slightly, from 10% to 12%[16].

The expectation that both partners should have an equal say in household financial decisions is already firmly entrenched in the majority of relationships. At current rates of change, couples will be reporting a completely equal say in financial decisions by around the year 2015 – that is to say the number of men and women who report having the final say will be equal, with the great majority (80%) reaching decisions by consensual negotiation[17].

OPENNESS ABOUT FINANCES: WHO CONTROLS THE TRUTH?

Equality and independence in financial control are both bound up with a further dimension, namely transparency. We found that one in 10 men do not know what their partner earns, compared with just one in 15 women. It seems that this relative openness about earnings was not always the case. Research in Britain in the early 1950s from the Mass Observation Archive found that around 20% of working-class women did not know what their husband earned[18]. Evidence from the same source suggests that some men had told their wives what they earned when they were first married, but kept subsequent pay rises a secret, keeping these for spending on themselves. The relationship between secrecy and control of spending was illustrated by one 40-year-old man in our research:

> My mother never knew how much my Dad earned . . . she'd have a certain amount of housekeeping and she'd have a part-time job and my brothers and sisters contributed but she would have to pay for everything. My father kept money for himself for drinking and horses.[19]

So, one of the biggest differences between now and the 1950s would appear to be the generally greater openness about money among today's couples. This may well be because there is more money to go round today, but must also be related to the fact that couples are much more likely to respect their partner's right to an equal say and degree of independence about money.

AVOIDING POLEMICS

Each generation since 1950 has had different aspirations and lifestyles from those of the previous generation, and the very fact of rapid social change introduces complexities into relationships between men and women. In Britain, and surely not untypically across the western world, more than two-thirds of men do more around the home than their fathers did, and a similar proportion of women do less housework than their mothers did. Figure 8.6 shows, perhaps unsurprisingly, that many people feel that life has been made more difficult for men as a result (but interestingly fewer think it has for women).

Therefore, it no longer makes sense for most people to appeal to gender role models to allocate tasks in the home. We have shown too that in the area of finance things might be more open but also less clear-cut. To a great extent arrangements must be renegotiated by every couple, depending on their individual circumstances. Both men and women have to cope with a less 'given' life course and a wider portfolio of potential roles and responsibilities. Yet for many, modern 'androgynous' ideals can seem

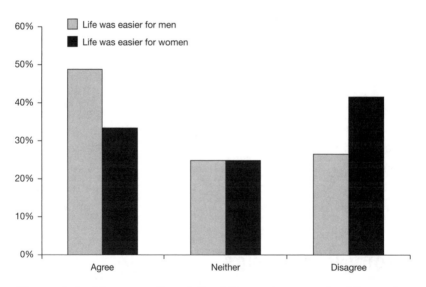

Figure 8.6 More complicated lives? Proportions agreeing/disagreeing that 'Life was easier for men/women when gender roles were more clearly defined'.

Source: nVision, Future Foundation.

impossibly demanding or irrelevant to present realities. For most, partnership and parenthood call for some tough compromises. Welcome though a move to gender equality might be, the reality is that it can make life more complicated.

Organizations need to avoid the polemics and prejudices that plague commentary on gender, so that they can get a clear understanding of the current impact of gender on the division of labour and its implications for the control and spending of money. There is already plenty of discussion of the new men and new women the gender revolution has produced, and plenty of rather blunt marketing characterizations of these new types. But marketers and product designers need to embrace a much more complex and sophisticated approach when it comes to understanding and responding to the actual day-to-day process of role redistribution and the complications it brings. New ways of looking at more flexible couple or family friendly offerings (especially in financial services as we noted earlier) are needed.

Segmentation along gender lines just gets harder – and more dangerous. In a world where younger men and women have increasingly similar outlooks and aspirations, marketers need to be wary of trading in ideas of 'new types' of men or women – in most cases these are best reserved for insults or comedy routines. Even invoking a degree of ironic distance won't refresh a stale gender stereotype or equally clichéd inversion. With so many 'gender-based' campaigns somewhat missing the mark, a sensitive, fine-grained and sociologically well-informed approach to men, women, and their relationships will be all the more effective.

CHAPTER 9

THE PARENTING CHALLENGE

A lot is expected of parents nowadays. The exhortations to take parenting and parental responsibilities seriously come not only from social commentators in the media but from government too, partly — it has to be said — to redirect the blame for failing schools, truancy and youth crime. At the same time, as we discuss in the next chapter, there is less fatalism now — so if an accident happens to a kid, or she or he 'goes wrong' in some way, then it is no longer just bad luck, it must be someone's fault, and parents will usually be the prime suspects. This, in part, explains the increasing anxiety we have as parents. In fact, it is not too extreme to wonder whether British sociologist Frank Furedi is right when he claims that our worries and our concerns, our desire to do right and be seen to be doing right, is leading to the development of what he calls 'paranoid parenting'.

> Most parents I know are not just worried about how they are performing as fathers and mothers: they are paranoid about it.[1]

PROFESSIONAL PARENTING VERGES ON THE PARANOID

For those people in the parenting stage (and remember that around 70% of people will become parents at some point) bringing up children is a major source of not only anxiety but also complication. Trying to be a great parent while maintaining other things (like a job, as increasing numbers of women do) not only promotes a sense (and a reality) of busyness but it makes life more complex to juggle and control. Nothing characterizes the complexities of modern life better than the trials and tribulations, the choices and decisions and the worries of today's parents. This has major implications for society and provides a spectrum of opportunities for organizations to help parents overcome the stresses and strains of modern family life. This might be through convenience products that make living easier, advisory and support services for parents, or products that support 'parenting' as an activity, especially those that support children's safe development and education (which, as we will show, parents increasingly worry about). Most of all, companies and public sector providers need to understand the reality of lives and the mindsets of today's professional, but somewhat paranoid, parents. In this chapter we look at four aspects of how parenting has become more complex:

- How parents are spending more time with their children (both in the home and out of it), especially in planned activities and educational support, as they strive to give them the best experiences, even at the cost of their own lives – what might be called the *professionalization of parenting*.
- How they are worrying more about their children on a range of dimensions – the development of the *paranoid parent*.
- How the rights and voice of children has increased so that they are more involved in family discussions – the growth of the *negotiated family*.

■   And finally, how parental responsibilities are increasingly being maintained even when the children grow up – *forever parents*.

PROFESSIONAL PARENTING

More time with children

On the face of it, parenting should be easier today than it has ever been. After all, the average family has fewer children and there is significantly greater provision of childcare and schooling. However, time-use studies in Britain reveal that parents in the 1990s were spending an average of 85 minutes a day per child concentrating on childcare, and this compares with a mere 25 minutes a day in the mid-1970s[2]. This is a massive increase, which far outweighs any time gained from today's relatively smaller families. In the United States, there has also been an increase, albeit to a smaller degree than in the United Kingdom. As Robinson and Godbey note: 'Per capita, in other words, 1980s children had slightly more parental time than children raised in the 1960s'[3].

Jonathan Gershuny and Kimberly Fisher, from the Institute for Social and Economic Research at the University of Essex, explain the factors behind the increase in childcare time in Britain:

> Time devoted to child-care (as a 'main activity') has increased regularly and substantially . . . (partly because of perception of increasing dangers to children; partly because of new child-raising concepts like 'quality time'; and partly because a reduction of core housework and cooking time allows the conversion of formerly 'secondary' childcare activities – e.g., preparing the supper while supervising the toddler – into primary activities).[4]

Our own research highlights why parents are giving so much more time to their children[5]. We found a clear sense of needing to work harder today to be good parents, to provide the best for your children both materially *and* in terms of involvement in their lives. The outcome is a much closer engagement by parents in children's lives, with a focus on maximizing their offspring's chances in what is seen as an increasingly demanding environment.

More engagement with children

Parents feel they spend more time with their children than their own parents had spent with them, be that discussing things, helping with homework or participating in leisure activities (Figure 9.1). Indeed, in every one of the aspects of parenting we explored, fewer than one in ten parents claimed to spend less time than their own parents had. In this sense, the vast majority of mothers and fathers feel they take parenting more seriously than their parents did.

Not surprisingly perhaps, those activities seeing the least change between generations are the more informal, spontaneous aspects of the relationship, talking together, or just having 'fun' or 'a laugh'. The biggest differences between this generation of parents

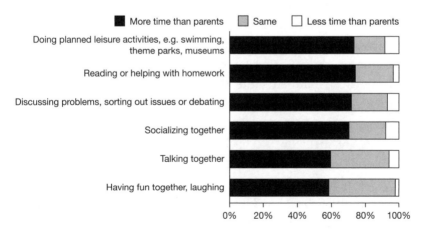

Figure 9.1 Spending time with children in various activities. By comparison with the amount of time respondents spent with their own parents

Source: *Complicated Lives Report*, Abbey National/Future Foundation.

and the previous one seem to be occurring in more deliberate activities: doing planned leisure activities and reading or helping with homework. So, much of this increased time spent on parenting is in actively engaging with the children: we discuss things more than in the past; we take them out to restaurants, cinemas and theme parks; and we help them with their school work to improve their chances of success in the future.

Keeping up appearances for the child's sake

But parents also want to ensure that their children do not suffer in comparison to others in the more material areas of life. Kids, more now than adults – who as we argued in Chapter 2 are moving beyond this in some ways – need to keep up with the Joneses, or at least the junior Joneses. This is reflected in the significant amounts of money that parents spend on presents and parties for children – both of which reflect the demands of youthful competitive consumption.

Certainly, parents believe that the quantity and quality of children's presents constituted one of the most striking differences from their own childhood[6]. The same is true of spending on birthday parties, which in Britain in 2001 amounted for some to a significant outlay – one in twenty parents spending over £200 and one in a hundred more than £500. And these are not just teenagers' parties (where one might expect an expensive event for a special occasion like reaching the age of 18) since the largest amounts are spent on the birthdays of children between the ages of 10 and 12[7].

How different this is from past times. Research conducted in Britain in 1950 by Mass Observation[8] provides a vivid picture of how meagre presents could be then:

> I gave savings stamps for the first birthday of my god-daughter and mother gave her some knitted woollies. (Woman, age not recorded.)

Nothing but an old army mess tin, rectangular, with two pieces of wire soldered on the bottom and four metal wheels attached, the whole rather hastily sprayed with weak red paint. (A father describes a toy his wife had bought for their child.)

A generation earlier, any sort of toy would have been considered a luxury. In the same Mass Observation survey, a 48-year-old housewife (talking about her own experience before the First World War) noted that 'we used to be given things needed in the house. I remember being given six cups and saucers when I was eight.' Another woman – a teacher – remembered that even though she had toys, 'Sunday was always a very happy day, because it was only then that we were allowed to play with our best toys'[9].

Of course, the growth in affluence is a critical issue here and this is recognized by parents, with 50% saying that this is the main reason why they spend more on their children than their parents did on them. But beyond this, there is clear evidence that peer pressure and competitive consumption is a factor, with one in four parents agreeing that this is the main motivation for spending so much on children's presents and parties[10]. In reality this is likely to be an underestimate, as many parents may be unwilling to admit to such motives.

Despite all the media commentary on parenting deficits (which we have shown is grossly exaggerated) and the guilt that might promote, there is little evidence that parents are lavishing presents on their children to compensate in this way. Only one in a hundred, in this survey, said it was the guilt factor – that they did not spend enough time with their children – that led to their increased spending in these areas.

Of course there are concerns that this increase in present giving and party spending is spoiling kids in some way. As one father we interviewed said:

Now they get presents all the time, they don't have to wait until their birthday or Christmas – like last year, them scooter things they just got one straight away – they don't respect it as much. Respect has gone out of the window because they get too much too quickly, they don't have to work for things.[11]

But, here is a classic example of the difficult position parents find themselves in. There are many – in the media and in politics particularly – who are keen to criticize parents, seemingly whatever they do. Some will complain that they do not spend enough on their children – that they are damaging them by not allowing them the thrills, experiences and belongings that other children have. (This form of relative deprivation is, after all, a main plank in the argument about child poverty[12].) Others will claim that by spoiling them, by giving them too much, they are endangering their development into adulthood (by failing to instil a proper understanding of money, values, responsibilities and hard work). Of course a balance between the two is needed but it is extremely hard for parents to know exactly what that is – just another of the many complications of parenting.

Putting the children first . . . and the relationship second

So parents spend more on their children, in terms of both time and money. And they do so, on the whole, because they are responsible, concerned parents who want to ensure that their offspring have the best of starts in life. But this concern for the children's well-being comes at a cost – the couple's relationship itself. For in devoting more time to their children, our research shows that, perhaps inevitably, there are fewer moments for the parents to have time for themselves – to be alone together. Let us be clear what we mean by this. It is not that family couples have less time together than they did in the past but it is certainly true that for many, they do not have as much time as they would like. With the development of more equal and emotionally close relationships between men and women – the 'companionate' or 'symmetrical' family as it has been labelled[13] – the time spent on outside pursuits and socializing by parents has actually risen significantly since the 1960s. But this is not as much as most couples would like in the 'have it all' world we discuss elsewhere. In the urge to pack so much into the average day the children clearly have first call on people's time. And this has major implications for businesses targeting family groups.

First, we have seen a decline in the time parents spend on 'hobby' activities – part of the explanation for this may well be that solo activities are being squeezed by the desire for close parent–child and couple relationships. On the other side of the coin, there are huge opportunities for 'double-coded' entertainment, which can be enjoyed by parents and children alike, but on different levels. Witness the major success of the *Harry Potter* series of books, or the relative recent fortunes of Dreamworks and Disney. (Arguably, Dreamworks has been prepared to risk taking 'double-coding' – and perhaps, in adult terms, a more radical politics – that bit further, with movies such as *Shrek*.) A further implication for retailers and leisure providers has long been recognized – the need for 'family-friendly' environments. Again, providing a safe and stimulating experience for adults and children to *share* is important, but as we shall see, the main chance may lie in providing for the possibility of a separate experience too – or a flexible combination of both.

The best way to illustrate the impact on a couple's time for themselves is to contrast their time-use with couples (of a similar age) that do not have children. This reveals that in Britain parents spend around 40 hours a week in their partner's company – about the same as non-parents – but that their children are present for two-thirds of that time. Thus, the parents only have only 14 hours on their own together – a mere third of the time available to those without children[14]. It is no surprise therefore that four out of five parents would like to spend more time with their partner[15].

These time-use data include time spent in the home as well as out of it but a similar pattern is true of away-from-home activity. Here, parents spend – as might be imagined – slightly less time out of the home with their partner than child-free couples do: two and a half hours per week as opposed to nearly three hours. Perhaps the most telling aspect here is that there is so little difference between the two – a reflection of the willingness and desire of modern-day parents to spend time and money taking their children to leisure facilities, to go out to eat or to go shopping, as we noted earlier. But the fact that parents do take their children with them when they venture out of the home means that they have little time – in fact only 50 minutes a week on average – to go as a couple to a restaurant, a bar or the cinema. No wonder that many parents feel the lack of time for going out (and particularly with their partner) is a difficulty, which creates the need for complex negotiations within and outside the household. And it is no surprise that satisfaction with social life has a particularly strong relation to satisfaction with life overall, and parents (especially new parents) tend to score low on both counts[16].

Part of the problem is childcare – finding someone who can look after the kids so that the parents can spend that essential quality time together. There is, of course, another solution that clearly many parents engage in – taking turns to go out on their own. Although this, in itself, is not necessarily a negative outcome (the majority of people agree that each partner can benefit from having some autonomy in their social life) it does require a degree of negotiation, particularly in a more egalitarian world, where gender roles are less specific (Chapter 8). So, the devotion to children not only squeezes the time couples can have alone together, but it increases the complexity of the whole process of deciding what to do and when and whether that be together or separately.

There is one final business implication of this – marketers should not assume that a parent is necessarily always 'constrained' by either the kids or the partner. We expect to see increasing interest in, and demand for, 'solo' activities. This already happens – the father going to a pottery class in the evening or the mother to the gym – but we expect it to continue to grow. Individual parents also already go out with a group of friends and will continue to do so, possibly to a greater degree. But this points to perhaps the most important conclusion – and one that is a constant theme throughout this book – that segmenting the population and making assumptions about attitudes and behaviour (in this case parents) will be increasingly difficult. When is a parent not a parent? That will be a more and more pertinent question in the future.

PARANOID PARENTING

So despite all the suggestions otherwise (by politicians and media commentators) all the evidence suggests that parents are taking parenting very seriously, and perhaps more assiduously than in the past. The danger here, and the complication, is that their own lives as individuals may be suffering, as we have just noted. But there is another aspect of parenting that adds complexity and also, potentially, has a negative impact on the children themselves. This is the excessive worry about a range of issues that seems to be an everyday part of modern life, as we discuss more fully in the next chapter. This manifests itself in particular reference to children and to such an extent that sociologist Frank Furedi has coined the phrase 'paranoid parenting' to describe it. Furedi's concern is that by over-worrying about our children's behaviour we risk the very thing we are most concerned about – their future prospects.

> In fact, probably the greatest casualty of the totalitarian regime of safety is the development of children's potential.[17]

Ironically, the majority of parents, at least in the United States, appear to agree with Furedi – in that they feel worried, in addition to everything else, about 'being over-protective'[18]. Important though this is (and it is an analysis that we agree with), it is not our direct interest here. Rather, we are concerned about how such views and such concerns add to the complexity of parents' lives. And they do so because more worries mean more apprehension about what is the right thing to do; it means more decisions. Parental anxieties can be categorized under three main areas:

- Making sure your child can develop the skills and opportunities to do well in life – *education* is critical here.
- Protecting their physical *health*.
- Ensuring their physical *safety*.

Education, education, education

The increasing concerns about education are understandable, particularly among middle-class parents who perhaps have a higher recognition of the importance of human capital in today's economic conditions, as we discussed in Chapter 4. You only need to contrast what people think and do today with opinions and actions in the past to recognize the scale of this change. In our discussions in Britain with different generations of the same family (grandparent, parent and adult child) the changing attitudes of parents in relation to schooling were clear[19]. There are choices to agonize over today that were rarely even considered in the past.

Whereas nowadays many parents take a very serious interest in which school their children might go to, this was not something that warranted much interest in the past. As one woman in her seventies said in our research 'All my children went to the local school . . . it wasn't an issue.'[20]

In a 1944 study of children's reading from the Mass Observation archive held at Sussex University, England[21], only 47% of adults said that their parents had encouraged them to read when they were youngsters, and an equal number said that they were not encouraged to read. The author of the report notes:

With very few exceptions those who replied in detail indicated that their parents had taken very little interest either way. Positive encouragement and positive discouragement both appear to be exceptional. Typical indifferent replies: . . .

'Nobody ever took any notice . . . No, I was only encouraged to work.'

One of the 1944 parents went so far as to say:

'Well, my younger boy always used to have his nose in a book. I had to stop him; he was getting indigestion and getting round-shouldered. I don't think it's healthy for children to read.'[22]

And, of course, attitudes to girls' education have changed tremendously. For many people in the past the issue of education for their daughters was, well not an issue. As one woman in her forties confided to us:

I always had the feeling that I was brought up to expect that I would marry a nice man and have children . . . I wasn't expected to have a career and worry about money.[23]

This increased concern about education manifests itself not only in the choices of which schools the children should go to, but in worrying about exams and homework (and more help with that as we showed earlier) and in greater visits to, and engagement with, the educational establishments themselves (for things like parents evenings). While much of this is to be welcomed, the impact on parents' stress levels and time-use is often underestimated. Also, of course, the concern about education has financial impacts too in direct fee-paying schools and universities (in some countries) and in 'top-up' coaching. So, parents worry more about education and are expected to be more involved in it. For a great many parents, this degree of involvement is something they never experienced in their own childhood, and it is something many feel anxious about. Business can do well by thinking broadly about the support services they can provide for parents as *educators*.

The health worries

Schooling is just one among many concerns which preoccupy today's parents – another is health. This ranges from concerns about minor ailments to fears about epidemics and even health procedures themselves. Thus, the number of parents in Britain refusing to allow their children to have the mumps, measles and rubella (MMR) vaccination has reached a crisis point in recent years following suggestions that it is linked with the development of autism (as yet unproved in the eyes of the vast majority of the medical profession). We do not wish to discuss here the reasons behind this behaviour as we discuss the whole concept of a 'culture of fear' in the next chapter. At this point, all we will do is leave this as an example of the growing health scares that parents are exposed to and have to deal with.

Another manifestation of such concerns is the greater readiness of parents to seek medical advice for more general, even mundane, complaints (somewhat paradoxical, given that professional opinion is ignored by many in the case of scares like MMR). This is particularly true for young children. Thus, in Britain, the number of National Health Service general practitioner consultations has risen for all age groups, but the sharpest rise has been for 0- to 15-year-olds (Figure 9.2). For the youngest, the average number of consultations per year has *increased* since 1972, from 4 to 6, meaning that average parents will have consulted a doctor about each child no less than 24 times in the first four years of her or his life.

Given that children are, on the whole, healthier than they were in the past, this must reflect increasing parental anxiety or a reduced ability to deal with the symptoms (cough, aches, pain) that the children themselves suffer. Professor Ray Tallis, professor of geriatric medicine of the University of Manchester, has commented that:

> The health of children cannot be getting worse. It must be something to do with the threshold at which we complain. We simply tolerate woe less well than we used to.[24]

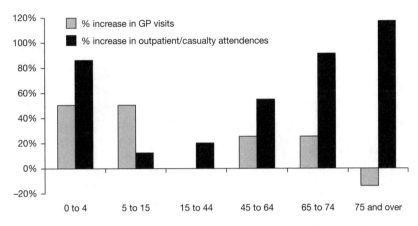

Figure 9.2   Visits to GPs and outpatient departments by age of patient. Percentage increase in visits to general practitioners and to outpatient/casualty departments, between 1972 and 2001.

Source: General Household Survey/Future Foundation.

The streets are not safe

A further aspect of concern is that parents are increasingly reluctant to compromise their children's safety by leaving them unsupervised. The result is that children are more mollycoddled than they were in the past and likely to remain dependent for longer. Research shows that in Britain before the Second World War the average age that children were allowed out to play in the street and to go to school alone was six. Yet, today's 18–25-year-olds were not allowed out to play until they were eight and did not go to school alone until the age of nine (Figure 9.3).

The bald average figures hide the true nature of change in the parental psyche. Contrast how one 70-year-old woman remembers what shopping was like 40 or 50 years ago, with one of today's parents:

> I used to park the pram outside Sainsbury's [a British supermarket chain]. . .there was a whole row of them . . . and I went inside and did my shopping.

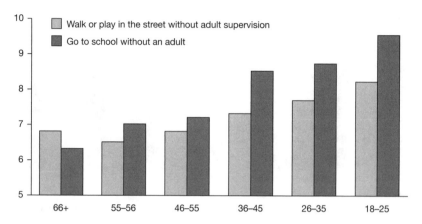

Figure 9.3 Independence comes later. Average age at which respondents were allowed to play in the street or go to school unsupervised, by age of respondent.

Source: *Complicated Lives Report*, Abbey National/Future Foundation.

(Children) can't play in the streets now . . . it's bad . . . got more traffic now and all these perverts . . . don't think you had so many before or at least we didn't know about them . . . we used to go out all day long.[25]

Given such concerns, it is little surprise that parents are turning to technological devices to help them supervise their children. The fact that children may well be in less danger today than they were in the past (Furedi claims that 'children are far healthier and safer than at any other time in history'[26]) is irrelevant – the critical thing is that parents worry more about them. So it should be no real revelation that many parents buy their children a mobile phone for security reasons or that they are keen on the prospect of other, as yet not readily available, devices for keeping an eye on their young ones. Figure 9.4 shows that fully three-quarters of parents in the United Kingdom would like to own 'an electronic bracelet' so that they could keep track of their kids at all times. (Whether the wearers would be so happy about this is another matter!) Four out of ten parents would like to have a video-link to their child's

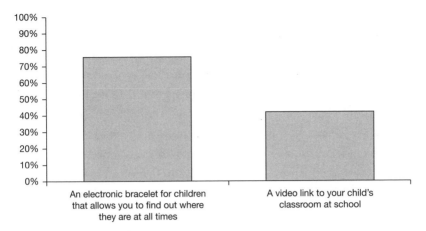

Figure 9.4 Parents' interest in owning child surveillance technologies. Per cent of respondents saying they would like to own the technology in question.

Source: nVision, Future Foundation.

classroom at school – something that has already been tried in the United States.

This suggests that technology has a significant potential to ease the concerns of today's paranoid parents. Already, as we noted, many parents and teenage children use the mobile phone to keep in touch to a far greater degree than would have been possible even five years ago. Photo messaging and videophones will provide another kind of surveillance for parents. There will be a downside of course. Communications technologies require collaboration from both parties, and thus are not about surveillance in the strictest sense, but will raise the familiar civil liberties question, (but now at an interpersonal level) – 'why switch it off if you have nothing to hide?'

Babies are routinely and uncontroversially placed under electronic surveillance, and we are seeing a gradual increase in the age at which this is acceptable, as systems for toddlers are now available which set off an alarm if they move outside a certain area.

Two-way radios, previously marketed as a play device for children, are now sold to parents as a way of keeping in touch with children while on excursions. Within the next decade, we may well begin to see children equipped with surveillance or communications technology at every stage during their growing up. The relationship between technologies of surveillance/contact and family life is already complex and interesting, and is sure to become a whole lot more so. And it presents obvious opportunities for technology companies who respond intelligently to the difficult moral, emotional and practical issues that such 'child surveillance' technologies are bound up with.

THE NEGOTIATED FAMILY

Another complication in modern family life is the increasing degree of negotiation that takes place. With more equality in the home (albeit not total), a weakening of gender stereotypes and a blurring of roles (as we discussed in Chapter 8) so more discussion is required between parents about who does what and when (as we noted earlier in relation to going out). But, such democracy in the home does not stop with the parents. Increasingly, children are involved in family decisions while at the same time being given greater leeway in their own consumer choices. These two aspects of what might be called the 'negotiated family' – democracy and personalized consumption – both increase the complexity of parental life.

The democratic family

In all this talk about paranoia and pressures it should be said that many of the trends we are discussing are generally positive. It is just that for mothers and fathers they make things less straightforward than they were in the past. Nothing illustrates this better than the nature of relationships and discussion within the family. The former are seen as closer and more equal than in previous generations; the latter more extensive and open.

In that sense, it is clear that the family is becoming more democratic. We have already shown (Figure 9.1) that parents feel they spend much more time than their own parents did in 'discussing problems, sorting out issues or debating'. But, as Figure 9.5 illustrates, this extends specifically to decisions like where to go on holiday (and even, in our own discussions with parents, with things like the choice of a new car or television) and to a more general perception of openness.

Indeed, children's right to 'be respected by their parents or guardians, and to be involved in decisions that affect themselves'[27] is now enshrined in the United Nations' convention on the rights of the child – a potent illustration of the modern commitment to 'family democracy'.

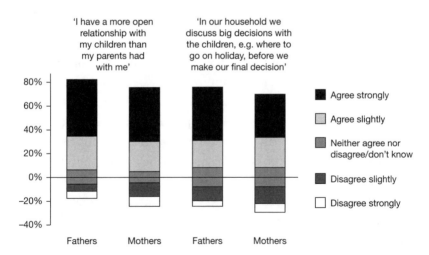

Figure 9.5 The democratic family. Agreement/disagreement with the statements, by gender of parents.

Source: *Complicated Lives Report*, Abbey National/Future Foundation.

Positive though this development is, it does, by its very nature, require more deliberation, more time and more negotiation. Decisions increasingly need to be cleared with others in the household, making them potentially more protracted.

Personalized consumption

At the same time as the range of consumer goods in shops and homes has increased (as we noted in Chapter 7), the movement towards economic equality and independent consumption within households has seen the role of shopper for the whole household become more complex and less likely to be the preserve of one family member. Even where one person is still responsible for household shopping, wider social trends make life more difficult. With the democratization of the family has come a *personalization* of consumption, making the family shopping all the more complicated. As a middle-aged mother said to us:

> I have to get different sorts of cereal for everyone, different sorts of shampoo, different sorts of coffee.[28]

Shopping for a family is less and less about shopping for a unit, and more about combining the lists of several individuals. Our consumer research reveals that the average household in Britain now has three different types of shampoo and three different breakfast cereals. Not only that, but particularly when they are young there will be major demands from the children, and serious debate with them, about what it is appropriate for them to have. Kids learn some key elements of negotiation at a very young age. Surely all parents at some time have heard the claim that 'Kate's mum lets her have . . .' or the equally ominous 'if I can have . . . I'll help you with the housework (or whatever)'. (They never do.) So, the very nature of children's consumption and household shopping becomes more complex.

Marketers need a clear picture of which areas of consumption children will make their own choices in, which parents will control, and which will be negotiated between them. Of course, this varies by market, and by the age of the children. But our research suggests that in Britain over 50% of kids are always or nearly always choosing what to do with their own time by the age of nine. For what clothes they wear out of school the equivalent age is 10 and with what to eat in the evening around 16.

FOREVER PARENTS

While parents spend more time with their children, worry more about them, are more engaged with them and have to go through the processes of negotiation more often than their parents did, surely they can look forward to a period of more freedom and fewer worries once the children have grown up and left home? Although the period after the kids have left home (the so-called 'empty nester' life-stage) is one where life satisfaction tends to be highest[29], it is not so simple as that. Our research suggests that adult children are relying on their parents more than they have ever done. Two aspects illustrate this point: continuing financial support and a growing likelihood of returning home at some later point in life.

Financial support

Figure 9.6 looks at two aspects of financial support parents can give to their children: help with housing costs and the saving of money for the children's future. Although the methodology is not ideal (older people may have simply forgotten what they received), the types of giving are sufficiently important – so most people are likely to remember the event. It can be seen that older generations were much less likely to receive financial support.

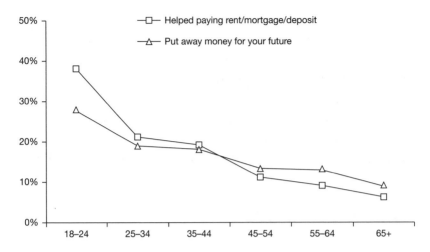

Figure 9.6 Financial support from parents. 'Which of the following, if any, did your parents ever do for you after you left home?' (Base: all aged 18+ who have ever left home.)

Source: *Complicated Lives Report*, Abbey National/Future Foundation.

The same pattern can be observed for other forms of financial support covered in this survey, with the proportion of each age group receiving help growing consistently as time has gone by. The only exception to the trend is receipt of large lump sums, where 25–34-year-olds are the most likely to have received these (perhaps to help them into the housing market) and a reflection of the fact that the youngest adults in the survey had not yet needed, or called for, this type of help.

Of course, parents have always provided financial support to their children but anecdotal evidence and these data (despite the caveats) suggest that this has become more important over time.

With parents providing increasing financial support to adult children in various ways, providers of services to families should not be disheartened by the demographic decline of the family household, as there is a clear opportunity to extend 'family cover' well beyond the point where children leave home. The same might apply to insurance (home or motor, for example), media subscriptions (magazines or television channels are some possibilities) or the area of housing where mortgage suppliers might 'tailor-make' products for 'family' ownership of a property, giving parents/children shared rights and responsibilities. There are obviously regulatory issues in some of these instances, which might be something a family-friendly government might want to look at.

The financial burden of adult children is exacerbated by a suggestion that in Britain children are delaying their departure from the family home compared with, say, the 1970s and 1980s. This has further financial implications for the parents.

But British families have it easy in this respect compared with those in some other countries. In Europe, Italy is leading the way with children (and male ones especially) staying at home. Many Italians, as in the rest of Europe (and indeed much of the developed world), are delaying getting married – up by an average of three years for both sexes since 1980. Clearly this is one aspect in young adults staying longer in the family home, but in Italy it cannot be the only factor in the phenomenon of '*Mama's Boys*' as they have been labelled by the Rome based Psychology Institute of the National Research Council.

Returning home

Not only are adult kids probably taking longer to leave the family abode but once they have gone, they are more likely to return.

Figure 9.7 looks at those who left home at the age of 20 or younger and shows that in Britain more adult children than ever are returning home again after leaving. Overall, taking all children who have ever left home but returned at some point the proportion has risen from a quarter to nearly a half between the late 1950s/early 1960s and today[30]. Part of the reason for this is the growing number of students going to university and, indeed,

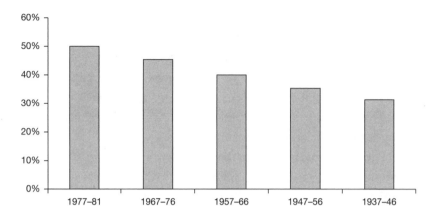

Figure 9.7   Returning home. Proportion of adults who had left home by age 20 and have returned at some point by year of birth.

Source: *Complicated Lives Report*, Abbey National/Future Foundation.

financial problems and higher education are the main reasons children are more likely to return home today.

So, parents are hit by a double whammy from their kids – not only do they spend more on them than previous generations when they are at home and in helping them live away from home *but* they are more likely to have to offer hotel services to them too! This applies nowadays to even quite mature offspring – break-ups of partnerships and marriage being a major reason that children return home after age 30.

This all adds to the complexity of parenting. Although in the past, support and financial help were provided (things have not changed in that respect) once children did leave home there was an expectation that they were then independent and needed to organize their own lives. Now parents have to worry not only that they might be called upon for significant financial help but that they need to keep extra rooms available in their homes should the prodigal son or daughter return. Of course many parents welcome them warmly but it does make life somewhat less easy to predict.

PARENTAL HELP

While the real and perceived difficulties of protecting and nurturing children may be increasing, the intricacies of involvement and interaction provide a potentially compensating benefit. Although it all makes for a much more complicated and involved kind of parenting, it is clear that there are real rewards for both parents and children.

Add in the expectation of parents to have a good social life and, for many, a successful career (or, more negatively, just the financial pressure of having to work) and the complications are multiplied. No wonder that life satisfaction is lower in the family age groups than at other points in life or, as Figure 9.8 shows, that satisfaction with life and the home increases on average when children move out (whereas for children the reverse is true). It is

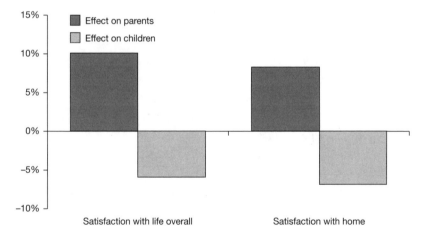

Figure 9.8 The psychological effect of children leaving home. Comparing responses in households in the year that children were in the home and the following year when they are no longer there. Percentage of parents/children whose satisfaction score increases, minus the percentage whose satisfaction score decreases.

Source: British Household Panel Study, Institute for Social and Economic Research, University of Essex/Future Foundation.

not, of course, that parents do not love or appreciate their kids but rather that it is just such hard and complicated work looking after them.

At the moment, there is little evidence that parents are changing their outlook or ambitions – they are still seeking to 'have it all'. This presents a potentially vast market for service providers and leisure venues who can respond to the tricky business of parents who do not want to compromise. Families are not only a key target market for convenience products and time-saving devices but they would welcome a whole range of other life-helping services: childcare, domestic services, training products for themselves (on parenting) and for their children (to assist them in their schooling). There could well be opportunities for financial products that are flexible enough to adjust to parents' changing needs over time or which make providing financial support to children easier (family accounts, for example).

But most of all, parents would welcome companies (and public services for that matter too) simply understanding and recognizing the complex issues and demands they face. This simple fact would be a good start for companies interested in this market and in Chapter 11 (on the issue of time) we provide some further pointers on this. Before that, though, we want to consider in more detail the anxieties and fears that not only parents but many other people face in the modern world.

CHAPTER 10

THE ANXIETY SOCIETY

How extraordinary! The richest, longest lived, best protected, most resourceful civilisation, with the highest degree of insight into its own technology, is on its way to becoming the most frightened.[1]

THE FEAR PARADOX

It is not only parenting, as we discussed in the last chapter, that people worry about nowadays. One of life's biggest complications – and one of the most paradoxical given the improvements to people's lives in the industrialized world over the last 50 years – is the growth in a wide variety of concerns. This is made worse by the difficulty people have in properly and rationally assessing risk. It seems that one of the consequences of a world of growing affluence is a sometimes irrational growth in anxiety about a range of life issues be they health, the environment, drugs, crime or terrorism. This truly makes for a more complex world – one where it becomes increasingly difficult for people to know which are the right life choices.

This phenomenon has been labelled (by two separate sociologists – one on either side of the Atlantic) as the development of *a culture of fear*. In Britain, Kent University academic Frank Furedi first described the concept in his 1997 book claiming that safety became 'the fundamental value of the 1990s'[2]. The paradox is that by most measures, the world is, at least for those in developed countries, a safer place to live in than it has ever been. (If this was not the case, of course, longevity would not have increased in the way it has done.)

Barry Glassner, professor of sociology at the University of Southern California, has charted exactly the same paradox in the United States in his book of the same name[3]. He argues that despite an objective and measurable improvement in many aspects of people's lives, there has been an increase in concerns, fears and hysteria – the same predominant pathology that Furedi identifies in Britain.

The trend is also evident across Europe, and indeed, the whole of the developed world, with important implications for business and government alike. First, and most generally, this is a deeply conservative force as it provides a catalyst for doubts in consumers' minds about new products or initiatives (for example, radiation scares with mobile phones and concern about the health and environmental impact of genetically modified organisms).

Second, it helps to foster volatility in markets for existing, sometimes well-established goods. This is particularly evident in the food and drink sector where health scares can occur suddenly, affecting sales dramatically. In recent years in Europe both Coca-Cola and Perrier have suffered when problems were discovered in their bottling plants. McDonald's blamed poor European sales towards the end of 2000 on consumer concerns over the bovine spongiform encephalopathy (BSE) outbreak in cattle herds which led to an albeit short-lived 27% fall in European beef consumption[4]. When the first case of BSE was confirmed in Italy in January 2001 (in an Italian slaughterhouse known to supply McDonald's) beef consumption fell by an estimated 40%[5] and the burger chain was particularly badly hit.

The fallout from BSE continues in Europe with French restaurant chain Buffalo Grill suffering from an investigation into alleged illegal importation of British beef during the crisis. In January 2003 (at least two years after the scare and some time after the ban on British beef was lifted) the group issued a profits warning and announced it was cutting investments and introducing a rigorous cost-savings plan[6]. The company's shares had been suspended the previous month after falling 90%.

Apart from just accepting this more mercurial world (where news and 'scares' travel even faster thanks to the Internet and other communication media), companies need to have in place mechanisms for anticipating and handling the potential impacts of this consumer 'pathology'. This includes research processes, crisis response strategies and the development of trust and goodwill through broader citizenship initiatives[7].

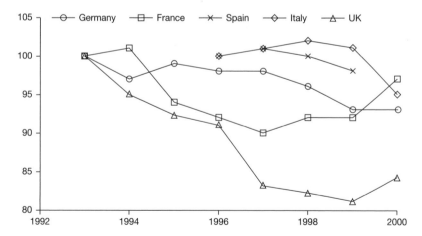

Figure 10.1 Crime – the true story. Total criminal offences across Europe – indexed where 1993 = 100.

Source: nVision Europe/countries' own statistical offices.

MYTHS OF SOCIAL AND ENVIRONMENTAL DECLINE

But it is not just food and health that is affected. Take, for example, attitudes to crime. Across Europe during the 1990s, crime rates were either stable or fell (Figure 10.1). This despite the fact that more crime tends to get recorded now thanks to an increase in insurance cover and, some have argued, the development of a 'victim culture'.

Yet, in 2000 56% of Europe's citizens feared an increase in drugs trafficking and international organized crime. Homicide rates have decreased steadily across the five major economies since the early 1990s although you would not have thought so given the concerns people express about personal safety. This all seems to mirror what Barry Glassner has observed in the United States[8]:

> Why are so many fears in the air, and so many of them unfounded? Why, as crime rates plunged throughout the 1990s, did two-thirds of Americans think they were soaring? How did it come about that by mid-decade 62 per cent of us described ourselves as 'truly desperate' about crime – almost twice as many as in the late 1980s, when crime rates were higher? . . .
>
> Give us a happy ending and we write a new disaster story.

This is merely one example of the phenomenon of a 'culture of fear' in which humanity seems destined to worry more and more about a range of issues, often even though things are getting measurably better. On a range of measures, as Furedi and Glassner show, the world is objectively a safer place to be (except, of course, and again paradoxically, in the increase in dangerous sporting activities).

Consider popular views about the environment. Things are getting worse are they not? Is there not more pollution, more poverty, more starvation, a running down of natural resources and a depletion of species? Certainly the public seems to think so – in a survey we conducted in June 2000, seven out of ten Britons agreed that air pollution was worse than it had been 50 years ago. But things are not as certain as they seem.

The quality of air in Britain is actually far better than it was in the 1950s when smogs, caused by the extensive burning of coal for heating, were a regular occurrence. On a broader level, the American Julian Simon in 1995, and more recently the Dane Bjorn Lomborg (2001) have argued rather persuasively that maybe things are not quite as bad as we are often led to believe. As Lomborg notes:

> We are not running out of energy and natural resources. There will be more and more food per head of the world's population. Fewer and fewer people are starving. In 1900 we lived for an average of 30 years; today we live for 67. According to the UN we have reduced poverty more in the last 50 years than we did in the preceding 500, and it has been reduced in practically every country.
>
> Global warming . . . is almost certainly taking place but . . . its total impact will not pose a devastating problem for our future. Nor will we lose 25–50 percent of all our species in our lifetime – in fact we are probably losing 0.7 per cent. Acid rain does not kill the forests and the air and water around us are becoming less polluted.[9]

Despite our worries (and despite the barrage of criticism from the environmental movement of first Simon, before his death, and more recently of Lomborg), there is strong evidence that, overall, air pollution has decreased, water quality has improved, world poverty is being addressed and stocks of many minerals and carbon fuels are at historic highs. Yes, problems remain. Lomborg, for example, says that man-made global warming is probably occurring with some potential negative impacts. Governments and companies could do more to help the environment. But, overall the news is not all bad, and in total, is arguably rather good. Yet, the vast majority of people believe that the environment is getting worse and, importantly, most feel it will continue to do so.

Of course, this concern for the environment partly reflects the fear of its impact on our own health. The air we breathe may make us ill, as might the water we drink or the food we eat. Viruses and bacteria might cut us down, with bio-terrorism adding a new threat. Yet, one of the most amazing developments of the last hundred years has been the improvements in health care and hence the massive reductions in life-threatening conditions. The decline in mortality rates at all ages shows that we are less likely to die from chronic illnesses – in other words that we are healthier. (A cloud on the horizon is the increasing level of obesity that could threaten the more than century long steady increase in life expectancy.)

Figure 10.2 shows that people are living longer[10]. (The noticeable dips in some countries around the First and Second World Wars reflect not only the deaths arising directly from the wars themselves but also infectious disease epidemics that coincided with the conflicts. This is most apparent with the infamous 'Spanish flu' epidemic which devastated France in particular.) And although there is some debate about it, a general view is emerging among experts that we are living not only longer, but healthier lives too.

But you would be hard pressed to believe this given the media coverage of health scares and other threats and 'risks'. (Furedi notes there was a six-fold increase in the term 'at risk' in British newspapers between 1994 and 2000.) We have, it seems, an enduring (and

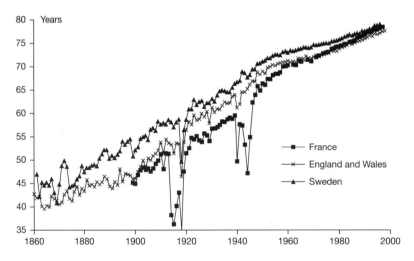

Figure 10.2 Improving health means longer lives. Life expectancy in selected countries.

Source: Human Mortality Database[11]/Vision.

morbid) fascination with being 'ill'. As we discuss later, people have a less fatalistic attitude to life – things do not happen by chance but because someone has made a mistake or we, as individuals, are not eating or doing the right things. And as we are exposed to and devour more information about our health and lifestyles, and as the symptoms and dreadful consequences of diseases are spelt out in detail in the media or on the Internet, so we worry more about them. All this is despite the fact that we have more doctors and spend more on health per head than at any time in history (Figure 10.3).

With more media comment, greater direct access to information that is not mediated by 'experts', a less fatalistic attitude and with reduced deference to institutions it seems that we have an inability to assess risk properly. It is not that we used to be any better at this, rather that we were more ignorant then and more prepared to believe what we were told. It is no surprise therefore that we have had such wild reactions to health scares like BSE, mobile phones and genetically modified organisms.

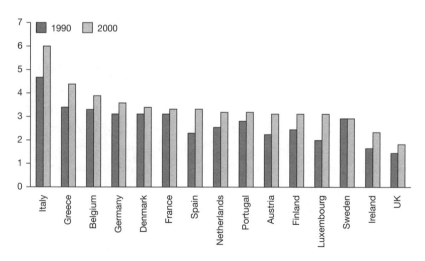

Figure 10.3 More doctors, more anxiety? Number of practising physicians per 1,000 population – 1990 and 2000.

Source: OECD Health Data 2002/nVision.

To confirm the essentially conservative nature of this 'fear' phenomenon we only need to look at the negative views about many new technology products. Despite no real scientific evidence that radiation from mobile telephones is indeed harmful, there has been a significant worry about this across Europe. (It is interesting to note that such concerns can be exploited – some might say cynically – by companies, with Levi's recently announced radiation protection pouch on a new range of jeans being an obvious example.)

Again, the rise of the Internet, e-mail and chat rooms has been presented by some as a dehumanizing, antisocial force, driving hordes of young people into atomistic, socially starved isolation. The reality, as both a Swiss study[12] and one in the UK shows, is that, if anything, the opposite is the case:

> In fact ... it appears that some aspects of sociability may actually be enhanced by web-use. It appears in particular that those who start to use the web, also actually increase the time they devote to out-of-home leisure activities such as cinema-going and eating out at restaurants.[13]

Indeed, our own work in Britain points to new communications technologies (and the old fixed-line telephone) actually increasing contact between family, friends and work colleagues. But to accept this fact, and rejoice in it, would not be seen as appropriate in the current moaning and anxiety-magnifying zeitgeist.

So, the value and safety of any technology is increasingly questioned. Technologies roll out and consumers purchase and use them but it seems inevitable that someone, somewhere will raise concerns about their impact on the social and physical health of society. And when the technologies are in development phase and are based on a science few people really understand, consumers' reticence is even higher. It is within this context that faith in the science behind, and efficacy of, biotechnology is declining, as Figure 10.4 shows.

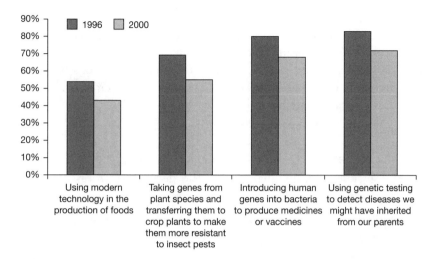

Figure 10.4 Declining faith in science, increasing scepticism? Percentage of Europeans mostly or totally agreeing that these applications are useful.

Source: Eurobarometer/nVision Europe.

So, we are seeing higher levels of concern across the developed world on issues ranging from the macro-political to the minutely personal. Unfounded though they may be, such concerns seem likely to continue to increase, and this has important implications for any organization, public or private, that depends upon the trust of the public. But in discussing these worries and the responses that they call for, it is necessary to understand what is behind this anxiety and growing hysteria – what is the cause of the 'culture of fear'?

WHY IS THIS HAPPENING?

Even behind the facades of security and prosperity, the possibilities of biological slippage and collapse are ever present. Hence the clinging and fear, even in the externally wealthy middle layers of society.

Whereas illness, addiction, unemployment and other deviations from the norm used to count as blows of fate, the emphasis today is on individual blame and responsibility.

Social problems can be directly turned into psychological dispositions: into guilt feelings, anxieties, conflicts and neuroses. . . . social crises appear as individual and are no longer − or are only very indirectly − perceived in their social dimension.[14]

As German sociologist Ulrich Beck has observed, one reason is the growth in individualism and the decline in group or institutional influence on individuals. Most people welcome increasing individual freedom but it comes at a price − it makes it clearer to people that they are in charge of their own destiny. So there is a reduction in fatalism and an emphasis on 'individual blame and responsibility'. Under such circumstances it is no surprise that we worry more about our and other individuals' actions.

Alongside the decline in fatalism has been a reduction in stoicism. We no longer accept that things just might happen to us by 'chance' and put up with it as a piece of bad luck. We now believe events should be controllable, accidents should not happen. No wonder people agonize about what to eat, the hidden danger of technology or the lifestyle activities they should engage in.

With people showing less deference to traditional institutions like the church, government or the medical profession, such establishment bodies not only have less influence (some would say control) on what individuals do in their day-to-day lives but there is clear evidence that people are more questioning of their authority and guidance. The scientific world might say a new technology is safe but can we really believe them? With a perception of increasing commercial influence on the scientific process, consumers are growing more cynical of companies' 'innovations' and more questioning of the independence of science. Trust in scientists as a professional body has remained reasonably high but doubts about their pronouncements on individual products or issues appear to be growing.

Part of the problem here has been a growing lack of trust in companies themselves, not helped by corporate cover-ups of scientific and medical evidence ranging from tobacco to asbestos to thalidomide to lead in petrol. More recently, there has been growing consumer concern over corporate use of science to manage or manipulate either markets (for example, 'terminator genes' in genetically modified crops that mean farmers have to buy new seeds each year) or life itself (patenting specific genes or gene therapy, for instance). The role of science in what has been presented as potentially apocalyptic developments has helped to undermine faith in science and thus rational thought.

This surely must partly explain the rise in health fads and fashions, most of which are based on only the flimsiest of evidence. If you cannot believe in science you might as well go back to witchcraft. In a devastating attack on many of the best-known alternative practices, Christopher Wanjek reveals the lack of scientific support for their efficacy[15]. Take, for example, herbal remedies, which are increasingly popular because, at the very least, they are natural and therefore should not be harmful. But as Wanjek points out:

> Poison ivy is natural but it is not something you would use in a skin cream. Mushrooms are natural, but half the species can kill you. Very potent yet common herbal remedies include mistletoe, comfrey and foxglove. These can all be deadly at even moderate doses, and you may be unaware of the true dose within each pill. So the claim that herbals are safe because they are natural is clearly false.

Worryingly, alternative medicines, like herbal ones, are not covered by the same degree of legal and professional control as mainstream medicine, yet many people go out and try them as soon as some new wonder 'cure' is announced. But not only are most of these alternatives proven to be ineffective, they could even be dangerous. As Wanjek says (again on the subject of herbal remedies):

The bottom line is that herbs, like everything else, are made of chemicals. Some chemicals are very safe for humans; some chemicals are very dangerous. . . . There is no logic in the idea that nature's chemicals are safer than a pharmaceutical company's chemicals. Thus, ingesting an untested herb is no different from ingesting an untested pharmaceutical.

We should not blame individual consumers too much as they do not necessarily have the means by which to judge whether the information they receive is correct or not. And, as we note later, it is hardly that they receive clear-cut advice from the media or even the scientific profession. Since there is less deference to authority figures, then inevitably the onus is placed on individuals to balance the evidence presented to them. But individuals do not have the skills – the basic mathematical and scientific training – to make proper (that is rational) judgements. As Ross Gittins, writing in *The Age* says: 'The wider point is that the public's lack of facility with basic maths causes it to be frequently misled by vested interests (and journalistic fools and knaves)'[16]. Melvin Benarde in his book *You've Been Had!: How the Media and Environmentalists Turned America into a Nation of Hypochondriacs*[17] proposes a national campaign to provide basic scientific education for all. Companies should not assume that such education is somebody else's business. While of course one cannot force information on people who are not interested, merely making it available is both reassuring (in line with a 'safety' brand) and a genuine expression of a broader commitment to social responsibility.

But that is not the only factor. Something else, something more worrying is taking place that we find hard to understand – people just seem obsessed with cranky, unproven ideas. Why accept uncritically the ideas of quacks (and it has to be said, people out to make a quick buck) but reject the ideas of science and established businesses? It just does not make sense. In his book *Health Food Junkies*[18], Steven Bratman highlights the dangers of an obsession with diets. He has coined a new phrase *Orthorexia nervosa* to describe a condition (that he suffered from himself) where people are obsessed, ultimately to the detriment of their own health, with what they believe to be healthy diets. Crazy.

Whatever the rights and wrongs of such behaviour, it clearly makes life more complicated. People, unsurprisingly, find it hard to know what is safe and what is not. And people seem to accept that this can change from month to month, week to week. One day coffee is bad for your health; the next it is good for you. One week alcohol is damaging; the next it will – in small quantities each day – make you live longer. One year fats are bad for you; then we are being told that they are positively good[19]. No wonder people are confused.

But perhaps the main reason why our anxieties are growing is that it is in some people's interests for it to do so. Barry Glassner identifies in his book three groups that have an interest in talking up concerns and fears: politicians, the media and advocacy (or campaigning) groups.

Politicians, and particularly those not currently in government, need to present the bad side of things to show how those currently in power are failing. Even incumbents sometimes talk up issues, particularly when they sense that there is a very real (if not always statistically supported) popular concern. Elections across Europe in 2002 saw tough talk from all sides of the political spectrum on the issues of crime and immigration.

As far as the media is concerned it has always been the case that 'bad' news sells better than 'good'. But, nowadays, with more media and more competition there is even greater pressure to 'embellish' stories to heighten anxieties. Melvin Benarde blames the media for creating 'an epidemic of anxiety, year after persistent year of alarm'[20]. It does appear that the media has a lot to answer for in many instances.

As Bjorn Lomborg notes, campaigning organizations quite naturally sometimes over-emphasize dangers to ensure they get media coverage and are better able to achieve their aims.

> Thus as the industry and farming organisations have an obvious interest in portraying the environment as just-fine and no-need-to-do-anything, the environmental organisations also have a clear interest in telling us that the environment is in a bad state, and that we need to act now. And the worse they can make this state appear, the easier it is for them to convince us we need to spend more money on the environment rather than hospitals, kindergartens, etc.[21]

One does not have to take a moral judgement on this as to whether the ends justify the means. All we need to note as objective analysts is that this does further help to create a feeling of a world that has gone wrong – to increase concerns. With so many more advocacy groups, and with more competition for media space and funds, this is clearly a factor in the development of a culture of fear, not least because such organizations tend to be trusted by the general public.

To these three catalysts to growing fears we can add two more. First, is business itself. This is not a major factor at present but indications are that it might become so. Cholesterol busting foods may indeed be a great addition to people's diets but the temptation to advertise them by highlighting the health dangers of cholesterol is all too obvious. A clearer example is Levi's new radiation protecting jeans mentioned earlier. Again, Levi's can quite legitimately claim that they are merely taking account of concerns expressed by their consumers and developing products to match. But, even though there is little real evidence yet of any serious health impacts from mobile phone usage, this – coming from a leading and respected global brand – clearly adds some legitimacy to the supposed threat. It seems likely that handset manufacturers are not too pleased by the stance taken by the American company.

Finally, there is the scientific community itself. With increasing pressure for funds and an increasing recognition that media profile might help in this, there is an understandable inclination to focus slightly more on worst case scenarios. For example, in September 2001 the BBC reported that scientists had noted a significant increase in the number of cases of variant Creutzfeldt–Jakob disease. Yet as Figure 10.5 shows, the annual growth rate of new cases had been declining for a year.

It turned out that the report was based on data that was a year old (when new cases did peak) but this only became clear later and not on the day of broadcast. A more recent example on the same subject was a study reported in September 2002 on tests on samples of tonsils and appendixes for the infectious agent responsible for vCJD. The test found one infected sample in the 8,300 tested, suggesting a possible range of infections across the whole population of anything between 25 and 45,000. Inevitably it was the top figure that tended to be reported in the media. To be fair, in this instance the scientist leading the study did make clear that there was too much uncertainty to draw any reliable conclusions (a comment that few media carried). But the net outcome was a request from government advisers for more research. One wonders though what would have happened if they had found no infected samples. It seems unlikely that it would

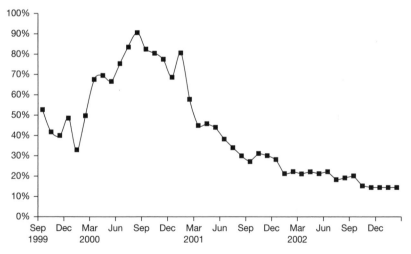

Figure 10.5 Growth in vCJD. Annual growth in new cases in the United Kingdom.

Source: Department of Health.

have been proclaimed that vCJD did not exist in the population at large (which would indeed be strange as over 100 people have already died from it) but it might have meant less impetus for more research. We are in no doubt that the study was conducted rigorously but the scientific community and society was, in a sense, fortunate that the one case was found since continued research is needed. But funding should not be contingent on generating fear and anxiety among the public. The right decision was made in this case but clearly it was easier to make given the scares surrounding the issue. But in an environment of fear, that might not always be the case if funding is diverted to less important research programmes on the basis of irrational concern, rather than rational analysis.

So the scientific community has a clear responsibility in maintaining complete objectivity and steering clear of any possibility of scare-mongering. It took a scientist (Sir Colin Berry, professor of morbid anatomy and histopathology, Queen Mary College, London in a speech to the Royal Institution in January 2002) to make the rather difficult point: '. . . some of us must avoid generating anxiety in order to increase our chance of getting our next grant.'

British doctor Michael Fitzpatrick made a similar point in reviewing *You've Been Had!* for the *British Medical Journal*. Commenting on Benarde's suggestion of a national science literacy campaign, Fitzpatrick said 'I think that this is a good idea, but suggest that rather than beginning with the schools, it should start where most health scares originate, in the medical establishment and the government'[22].

IMPLICATIONS

The emergence of a 'culture of fear', of increased worries and anxieties clearly makes life more complicated. Perversely, given that we are living longer, healthier and safer lives, we seem to have more to worry about, more to weigh up, more decisions to make. This has a number of implications for companies and governments alike.

First, it is important to accept that volatility in consumer behaviour is now a fact of life, and may well increase in future. This together with the need to understand that consumers are not necessarily rational operators suggests two things: planning is much harder and fluctuations in market shares and attitudes to products and brands likely to be greater.

Also, although other research we have conducted suggests that consumers embrace, and indeed in some instances welcome, innovation, do not presume that everything an organization does will be accepted. This expectation of progress is countered by a deep cynicism that borders on conservatism. This strange mix helps to heighten the volatility just mentioned.

This all suggests that companies need to be aware of some of the broader social, economic and political issues of our time. Understanding and analyzing these can help in the anticipation of problems ahead that might affect an industry or company.

It is also important to be prepared by having crisis management systems in place that can quickly tackle problems and develop responses as they arise. This clearly holds true for most fast-moving consumer goods producers and retailers but is not limited to them alone. In this irrational world any company can be engulfed in a supposed scandal of some sort.

Part of this process includes engaging in and developing dialogues with key stakeholders and players – whether they be customers, employees, relevant campaigning groups or government. Crises can be more quickly handled when communication lines are already in place.

Finally, it is important for an organization to build a bank of goodwill – building trust. One way of doing this is to become a citizen brand[23]. A 'good' company is given more leeway and more time to respond to actual or perceived mistakes and it has more credibility when addressing scares or 'scandals'.

CHAPTER 11

COMPLICATED TIMES

We cannot complete an analysis of the complexity of modern-day life without addressing the issue of time. Most, if not all, of the complications we have discussed are forged in the blast furnace of busy lives that voraciously consume *time*, sucking it in and constantly hungering for more. In fact, this is no coincidence for, as Gary Becker noted, 'The cost of time rises with rising productivity (the quantity of goods offered for consumption rises, and hence so does consumption itself, which also takes time); time thus tends to become scarcer, while the scarcity of goods diminishes'[1]. Furthermore, many writers have commented on how the very way people perceive time has changed, with the development of economies (away from agriculture and agricultural time[2]), the invention of the clock[3], and the move towards a 24-hour society[4]. All, in their own way, have helped to reinforce the feeling that we are busier now than we have ever been. So, time – and our use (or misuse) of it – has in itself helped to make life feel more complex.

THE VALUE OF TIME

Looking at time-use is the final piece of the jigsaw in under-standing what makes people's lives more complicated and in what ways. But this also provides further pointers to what can be done about it. By understanding time, we can start to consider direct solutions to the problems of complexity in the 21st century. In this chapter, we look at the reality of time – what is really happening – and the reasons why it seems such a problem. Most importantly, we propose a way of thinking about time – an equa-tion if you like – that will help us as individuals and businesses develop solutions to the time pressures many of us feel. We start, though, with exposing some of the myths about time, beginning with the world of work.

OVERWORKED OR NOT – TRENDS IN PAID WORK

Understanding trends in the time spent at work is important. Increasing work time is generally blamed for much of the busyness that people report in life. There is the implication that our free, or discretionary, time (calculated by deducting sleep and paid and unpaid work from the total of 24 hours in a day) has been eaten away.

Despite popular misconceptions that people are working longer hours in paid employment, the reality is that work time has almost certainly decreased. Although numerous writers have now argued this point[5], the idea of an increasing work 'burden' remains a constant refrain in the media. Yet, Figure 11.1 shows that work hours have decreased somewhat in countries across Europe in recent years.

But the idea that we are working harder now generally relies on a contrast with a more distant, soft-focus past. Yet if we take a longer view – for example, since the 1950s or 1960s – it is even clearer that work time has decreased, and quite dramatically too. In

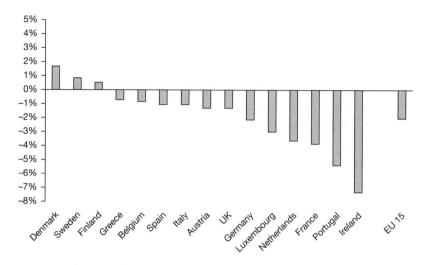

Figure 11.1 Working time across Europe. Change 1995–2001: all workers.

Source: Labour Force Survey/nVision.

America, Robinson and Godbey report that the time men spent at work fell by around 10% between 1965 and 1995[6]. Jonathan Gershuny's analysis of time diary data from 20 countries around the world shows a similar pattern[7]. Figure 11.2 splits the results by the level of education of male workers and shows that it is the less well-educated (and presumably, therefore, those in unskilled or lower skilled jobs) who have seen the largest reduction in work hours: by around a quarter between the 1960s and the late 1980s/early 1990s. One reason for this dramatic fall has been not only a decline in weekly hours and a growth in part-time work, but also an increase in holiday allowances. The impact of this is shown in the second part of the chart, which plots the average minutes per day for those days that people are in work. Now we can see that those with the highest educational qualifications (above secondary, and thus those most likely to be in managerial and professional jobs) have, indeed, seen their average working day increase slightly. This may explain the perception that people are working longer hours. First, for some

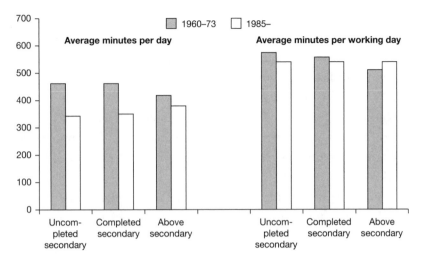

Figure 11.2   Time spent in paid work. Average minutes of paid work for men by educational attainment – 20 countries.

Source: Authors' analysis of Gershuny, *Changing Times*[8].

people on the days that they are in work, they are there for longer. Second, this particularly affects opinion formers and the chattering classes and may therefore get more media coverage – thus, we are all told that we are working harder, when in fact this is true only for some of us, some of the time.

Many factors are making our understanding of working time difficult. More women are working and therefore their hours of paid work are increasing overall. Against that, more people (and many of these new working women) are in part-time jobs that decrease average work time. There are more self-employed people, who historically have worked longer hours, while there is an increase in the growing knowledge economy in professional and creative occupations that can have long hours and tight personal deadlines (the 'hollywoodization' of work that we highlighted in an earlier chapter). But what cannot be disputed is that the 'average' worker, in the course of the entire year (in other words taking account of holidays and other non-work days), is not doing more hours than they did 30 or 40 years ago. Indeed they are working slightly less. (Analysis of time diaries from six industrialized countries finds women spending more time at work but men spending significantly less[9]).

Why, then, do people feel they are working longer hours? Robinson and Godbey show that when asked retrospectively how many hours they have worked in the last week (as opposed to filling in daily time diaries) people exaggerate the number of hours worked.

But there is a broader point than this mis-estimation by people of what they are doing with their time that goes to the heart of the 'wanting it all' debate. As Robinson and Godbey themselves ask:

> Whether it can be said that America is making 'progress' if workers are working somewhat shorter hours but estimate they are working longer is left to the reader. The additional free time that may result represents opportunities for life outside work that Americans have simply rushed past.[10]

Part of the reason people feel they are working longer is, as we said, that the media often tells them so. But we suggest it also represents a frustration, an irritation, with the rest of their lives – that people have so much more they want to do now than they did in the past. And work gets in the way of this. This is the source, we argue, of the whole work–life balance debate. People want, as we suggested in Chapter 2, to have it all. They want to participate in an ever-growing range of activities.

UNPAID WORK – THE CHORES OF LIFE

But before looking at the evidence of this desire for a wider and more extensive range of (leisure) activities, we need to look at the other main component of people's time-use – unpaid work. This includes housework, childcare, shopping and the like.

Obviously, many such activities are rarely seen as enjoyable, let alone fulfilling. But there are equally obvious exceptions: spending time with children can be hugely rewarding and pleasurable; and for many people shopping, even in some cases grocery shopping, is seen as a satisfying leisure activity. That said, one way that more free time can be released to ease the stresses presented by the search for a full and rewarding life is to spend less time on domestic tasks. This is doubly important since our research shows that household chores are a major source of irritation.

Figure 11.3 shows that many people, perhaps unsurprisingly, find the very process of keeping the house tidy an irritant. There seem to be close links here with children and the working status of parents. Whereas only four out of ten childless people got irritated, a full two-thirds of parents with 12- to 15-year-old children found tidying an irritation. However, the most annoyed people of all were found in households where both partners worked full-time and had children: seven out of ten of these people were annoyed by this particular chore.

The second most irritating thing for people (from the list of seven items we provided) was choosing what to eat, where one

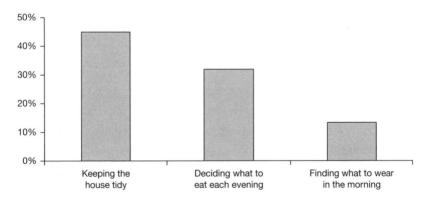

Figure 11.3 Household irritations. Which of the following often irritate you in your life?

Source: *Complicated Lives Report*, Abbey National/Future Foundation.

in three agreed this often bothered them. Again it appears that children play a vital part, with over half of those with 12 to 15-year-olds admitting this compared with only a quarter of those without children. It is the more mundane tasks of household management that create problems, and especially in those households where the combined pressures of family and work also exist.

But this is not the whole story. On the whole, it is young people who seem to have more irritations. The percentage of people who were not irritated by anything on the list grew continuously, from 9% of 18 to 25-year-olds to 46% of those aged 65 or over. Clearly, 'having it all' was never meant to include having to tidy up afterwards!

The growing intolerance of each successive generation for housework is put into starker contrast when we consider that in terms of housekeeping and cleanliness our expectations actually appear to be higher now than they were in the past:

> We used to have a bath once a week and otherwise we would have what we called 'a good wash' everyday . . .we wouldn't wash our clothes every time we wore them and we didn't have deodorant, we sewed bits of plastic under our arms to stop the material rotting. (Woman in her seventies.)[11]

> My daughter will only wear her jeans once . . . they have to be clean on. (Woman in her forties talking about her daughter.)[12]

Clearly, the proliferation of washing machines and much better stocked wardrobes have encouraged us to be more profligate in our usage of them and this is one of the reasons why technological innovation in the home has not reduced the time spent on household chores as much as might be expected.

But given that domestic tasks like the one discussed above are seen as less than rewarding it is no surprise that the time spent on non-paid work has decreased over the last 40 years. Figure 11.4 presents the combined data from six countries in North America and Europe[13]. It shows that the amount of core domestic

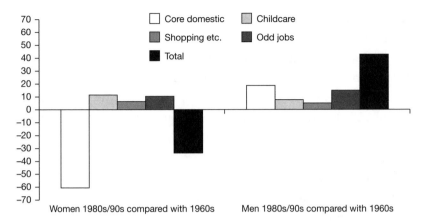

Figure 11.4   Time spent on unpaid work. Change in minutes per day across six countries.

Source: Jonathan Gershuny, Institute for Social and Economic Research[14].

housework has declined significantly for women (while going up slightly for men – who still, despite this, spend a lot less time in total on this activity). But this has been countered by more time spent on childcare, shopping and odd jobs (which includes home improvements – often now seen as a leisure activity). Overall, non-paid work time for women has decreased; for men it has increased.

A LIFE OF LEISURE?

The problem with looking at non-paid work in this way, as we have already made clear, is that some of these activities that are grouped under unpaid work time could, in fact, be counted as leisure (or at least pleasurable) pursuits. So, if there has been, on this classification, a slight increase in unpaid 'work' time, we have to recognize that this is largely work we freely choose to do, and thus the conclusion drawn by the authors of this study, that leisure time has stayed more-or-less constant in the last few decades, should be interpreted as the most cautious possible estimate. No serious commentator is suggesting that leisure time has actually diminished.

Research in America suggests, however, that 'free time' (as Robinson and Godbey describe it) increased by about six hours a week between 1965 and 1995[15]. Separate work in Britain finds a similar, if less dramatic change, with an estimated rise in leisure time of 20 minutes a day over the last 35 years (with women getting the main gain)[16]. This then raises the enduring question: 'why do people feel more pressured and that they have *less* leisure time?' As Gershuny and Sullivan note when discussing the American results:

> Robinson ... shows that there has been an increase in free time for both men and women, but makes the point that, significantly, this fact is not reflected in people's estimations of the way in which their time has changed.[17]

Part of the reason must surely be that the number of activities participated in has grown much faster than the growth in time freed from paid and unpaid work. We all want to enjoy a wider range of leisure pursuits. Indeed, as we argued earlier, there is an argument that what we do in our leisure time – the cultural activities that we pursue and the cultural capital that we accumulate – is becoming more critical in terms of how we, and society, view an individual. Certainly our UK data show that the aggregate number of leisure activities participated in has increased by over 20% since 1970 (Figure 11.5). (Note the greater increase for the 40-plus group, an important observation given some our points in Chapter 5 on the middle-ageing population.)

This is interesting since the amount of leisure time has only increased by 7% over that period. Either people have a wider portfolio of activities but on average do them less often during the course of a year (the question in the chart merely asks whether people have done the activity in the last 12 months). Or the average duration of each activity has decreased or shorter

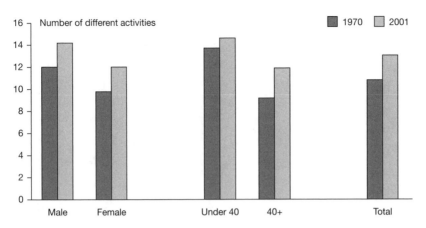

Figure 11.5   Increasing leisure portfolios. Number of different leisure activities people engage in during a 12-month period (in the South East of England).

Source: nVision, Future Foundation/*The Symmetrical Family*[18].

duration activities (like going to the gym or playing five-a-side football) have replaced longer duration ones like going fishing, knitting a sweater or playing a cricket match. Anecdotal and research evidence suggests both are happening, and this is clearly part of a broader process of 'de-routinization' of life. Where in the past, activities tended to take place in a more ordered sequence, and at set times and places, they are increasingly sporadic, unpredictable, 'snacky' and layered on top of one another. There is no better illustration of this than family mealtimes.

As Figure 11.6 shows, the very idea of the 'mealtime' is becoming increasingly redundant – something for media planners to chew on. While many families do still congregate to eat in the evening, the time at which this occurs is much more variable, and the length of time that the main meal occupies much shorter. This is supplemented by numerous episodes of snacking, most of which take place in conjunction with other leisure activities, especially watching television. This brings us to a further solution to the pressure on time – multi-tasking, a phenomenon that has been

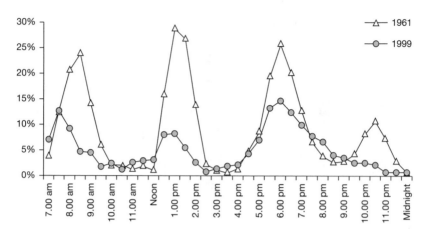

Figure 11.6   Snacky families. Proportion of parents engaged in eating at home, by time of day, 1961 and 1999.

Source: Future Foundation/Institute for Social and Economic Research.

highlighted by James Gleick[19]. As Robinson and Godbey note, this is particularly relevant to media consumption: radio listening used to be an absorbing experience, which people would often engage in to the exclusion of other activities, whereas 'today, radio is almost exclusively a secondary activity, something we listen to while doing something else. Television is beginning to go the same route. . .'[20]. The net result of our wider and more flexible engagement with leisure activities is almost paradoxical though. One of the reasons why we feel so busy and harried is that we desire to have a fulfilling, exciting and balanced leisure portfolio. This is a classic example of the greater complications in life.

But can we honestly argue that because we now have the financial discretion and the social freedom to engage in an increasing range of leisure activities that are now available that life is somehow worse? Do we really believe that people want or could go back to an era where life choices were more restrictive? Of course not, but we do believe that people seek, even ache for, help in managing their more complex lives and leisure portfolios.

ASSESSING THE VALUE OF TIME

In this way, the management of time becomes a critical factor in dealing with more complicated lives. But, how do we allocate time? How do we trade-off the time between one activity and another – which we must do if there is simply not enough time to get everything done? To understand this, we need to think of the processes by which people allocate time to different activities – we need to develop a theory of time.

In his book *Busy Bodies*[21], American economist/urban planner Lee Burns argues that time, and the management of it, has now become the most important driver of social change and innovation. For Burns, nearly all technological and social innovations over the last 50 years (from the microwave oven to changing religious and sexual behaviour) can be attributed to a desire to maximize the use of time. He argues that people can do this in two ways: either by increasing the *satisfaction* gained from any given unit of time or by *reducing the amount of time* to achieve the same amount of satis-faction. Burns concentrates on people increasing the ratio of satisfaction to time by reducing the minutes or hours spent on any activity, and his conclusion is that in the rush to get things done ever more quickly we experience the 'paradox of the good life': a more frantic and less satisfactory life despite greater affluence.

If we did all focus on reducing the amount of time on an activity at the expense of all else it would lead to that frantic, ever-faster world that Burns portrays but fortunately that is not what we all do, all of the time. Sometimes, we try to get more satisfaction from the same unit of time. We might take as long over a meal at a restaurant, for example, but gain more satisfac-tion because the food or ambience were better than the 'normal' place we go. Equally, we might sometimes gain satisfaction from deliberately taking a long and leisurely time to do things, just as a counter-balance to the hectic pace of the rest of our lives. Think here of anything from flopping in front of the television after a hard day's work, to the beach holiday where the whole point is to relax, read a book and do very little else (except get bronzed of course).

So, adjusting the ratio of satisfaction to time spent is more complex than simply offering 'convenience'. First, it has to be remembered that not all people are time-pressured and that for those that are not, the numerator of the ratio (satisfaction) will be more important than the denominator (time). Second, even for those people who are extremely time-pressured there are those situations where they might feel they can increase their satisfaction by slowing down the pace of life and increasing the time they spend on the odd activity – a sort of 'time oasis', like the beach holiday just described.

To understand how we might help people with their perceived time pressures, we thus need to think more about this satisfaction to time ratio – we need a theory. For this, let us start by defining the ratio thus:

$$(Time) \ R(atio) = S(atisfaction)/T(ime)$$

And, we can agree with Lee Burns that most people are trying to maximize their ratios. But this might not come, as Burns emphasized, just by reducing time (although that will happen in some instances); it might come from seeking to increase satisfaction. But the satisfaction from any activity is likely to be a function of people's needs (ranging from cleaning to cooking to relaxing to seeking thrills), their mood and, critically, on the outcome – whether the activity itself was a success. (You might have spent a lot on the meal but the service was poor; you could have gone to an outdoor sports event but the weather was bad; you might have gone reluctantly to the cinema to see a film and been positively enthralled by it.) This can be represented by the following formula:

$$S = f(Need, Mood, Outcome)$$

But, we know that what you want to do (your need) is affected by who you are, where you are and when you are there. Your age, but more often (as we showed in Chapter 5) you life-stage, will affect what you want to do. Parents have a range of specific activities that result from the very fact they have children – from the pleasant (playing with them) to the less so (clearing up after they have made a mess). Circumstances like how well off you are or the size of your home will have an impact too. And, of course, we are all individuals with our own personalities and interests. Then, where you are (at work, at home or in the shopping mall) and the time you are there will also determine what you want or need to do. So,

Need = f(life-stage, circumstance, personality, time, place)

Your mood will also be a function of your personality, and the time and the place and thus we represent this as:

Mood = f(personality, time, place)

Finally, the outcome depends on what actually happens (in a leisure or purchasing environment, the quality of the experience) but also on your expectation before engaging in the activity. How often has something been a pleasant surprise when it was better than you expected, and hence seen as a satisfactory experience (a high ratio). Thus:

Outcome = f(actual experience, expectation)

Immediately, this highlights a number of potential implications. Given its occurrence in a number of the formulae, it is clear that the context of an activity – the time and place and whom you are with is very important. Businesses need to recognize this fact and build offers and segmentation around the recognition that the same person will sometimes want different things on different occasions. Marketing activity often needs to be occasion-based. Another observation is that if something is oversold then the degree of disappointment is likely to be higher. Of course the benefits of an activity – the good points about it – must be communicated to a potential consumer but an overblown and downright misleading description is likely to end in a disgruntled customer. This is a problem that has afflicted the package holiday industry with the nightmare of the hotel next to a building site and miles from the beach being just one example.

But, without wishing to strain the theory beyond its value, we can take it further. Particularly where leisure is concerned we might be able to assume that people take a broadly based view of things and are trying to maximize the total value of the ratios across their activities. In other words:

$$\text{People seek to maximize } \Sigma \text{ R}$$

There are a number of ways that people might do this. First, we can hedge our bets – the more activities you do, the less likely one bad one will spoil your day, week, month or year. Second, it may be that the pleasure gained from doing an activity again and again reduces the more you do it, so you look for new and more exciting things to do. (There is an alternative case, of course, where the satisfaction increases the more skilled you become in an activity. Just think of the people who spend huge amounts of time playing golf, windsurfing or skiing.) Finally, people might feel that participating in a wider range of pursuits increases their cultural capital. Whatever the reason, we have already shown that there has been an increase in the average number of different leisure activities that people participate in.

IN SEARCH OF HAPPINESS

There is a strong argument that people's leisure activities are an important factor in determining overall happiness. Happiness – and hedonistic psychology as the study of happiness is called – has become a fashionable issue as incomes rise and people discuss what post-materialism means. And a formula for happiness has been proposed:

$$\text{Happiness} = f(\text{leisure, valued consumption}) + \text{rank}^{22}$$

In this, a person's overall well-being depends on their leisure time and activities, on enjoyable consumption (the valued consumption component) but also on income and consumption that confer status (rank). We should recognize that for most people, work in itself (including travel to and from it), does not contribute greatly to happiness as Table 11.1 shows.

But the hours spent at work do provide the money that can be used to fund consumption or leisure. In this way the use of time, and the way we trade it off, is critical in determining how happy we are. We can use that time to earn more money so that we can own or do more things but that in turn reduces (because time is a finite resource) what is available for doing those things. This is where the stress comes from. And in a society where what you do (cultural capital) and who you mix with (social capital – see Chapter 4) are becoming more important than what you own then this trade-off between work and leisure activities becomes more complex. In the terms used above leisure is becoming more important than consumption in determining rank. Because status is now not only gained from your job and income but also from your lifestyle/leisure choices, then getting the maximal balance is harder to calculate.

Table 11.1 Satisfaction from different activities. One thousand working women in Texas were asked to divide the previous day into episodes and to note how long it lasted and how happy they were.

Activity	Happiness (index)	Average hours per day
Sex	4.7	0.2
Socializing after work	4.1	1.1
Dinner	4.0	0.8
Relaxing	3.9	2.2
Lunch	3.9	0.6
Exercising	3.8	0.2
Praying	3.8	0.5
Socializing at work	3.8	1.1
Watching TV	3.6	2.2
Phone at home	3.5	0.9
Napping	3.3	0.9
Cooking	3.2	1.1
Shopping	3.2	0.4
Computer at home	3.1	0.5
Housework	3.0	1.1
Childcare	3.0	1.1
Evening commute	2.8	0.6
Working	2.7	6.9
Morning commute	2.0	0.4

Source: Kahneman et al. (2003), quoted in Professor Richard Layard's 2003 Lionel Robbins Memorial Lectures at the London School of Economics.

But the implication of this train of thought is that, on the whole, we need to work somewhat less if we are to have time to develop the all important embodied capitals. Indeed, we suspect that most people would readily trade lower work hours for more leisure but cannot do so because of employer pressure and the general trend in society and the business world for faster and faster turnaround. In fact, we expect the reason why people feel they are working longer than they actually are (as we noted earlier) is for this very reason – they know they are working longer than they want to.

Writing about happiness in the *Financial Times* Richard Tomkins makes the point that in a hundred years we could be 19 times better off than we are now[23]. He asks, quite rightly:

> And how would we use our enormous wealth? Would we all have 19 times as many cars, 19 times as many houses and our own little fleets of private jets and yachts? Where would we put them all? Would we have 19 times as many vacations? *How would we find time to take them,* and where would we find a corner of the world that remained unspoiled by fellow vacationers? [Our emphasis]

In a way Tomkins reinforces our point. As affluence grows there is a limit to how many material goods people can, or will want to, own. But the money could and will be spent on less tangible leisure and other services (and mostly by improving their quality) but the constraint will be time. However rich we are, we cannot stretch time (except, as we point out later by living longer). People will be juggling a set of aspirations and ambitions trying to get the best balance between work and leisure and between leisure activities themselves.

The result is that there are a number of strategies people can employ (we assess what this means for service providers later):

1. They will seek to reduce lower satisfaction activities (those towards the bottom of Table 11.1) or those with low time ratios.
2. They will try to balance work time with leisure time to maximize happiness.
3. They will tempted towards higher satisfaction activities.
4. There will be special interest in 'cultural' activities that provide not only pleasure but status too.
5. In general, they will try to increase the time ratios of any particular activity by:
   - wanting to do chores quicker: to reduce the T for the same S;
   - wanting more 'intense' experiences – to pack more in, in a shorter period of time: to increase the S for the same T;

- but they might also want to 'redefine' time: it is possible to increase satisfaction by 'slowing down' time – our beach example again;
- or they may combine activities or reclassify them – thus, chore shopping could be made more fun or a chore activity could be combined with a more satisfying one (having your dry cleaning done while you are at the cinema).

6. Finally, people are likely to continue to try to shift time or overcome the constraints to when or where they might do things. The consumer drive behind the 24-hour society is a case in point. By removing time markers the 24-hour society provides more flexibility, allowing people to manage their time more productively. For example, in some research we conducted a couple described the gains of being able to do their grocery shopping late at night. At night the shops were less crowded and so shopping was a quicker and more pleasurable experience – their satisfaction to time ratio had improved. By freeing their Saturday morning, when they had previously done their shopping, it also released time for more pleasurable family leisure pursuits – in other words it improved the satisfaction to time ratio for Saturday morning too. A double whammy!

How does this help us understand consumers' complications? It does so because time gives us a metric by which to measure complications – they arise, as we have shown, in part from people wanting to do too much. And it highlights the following issues that business needs to embrace.

THE BUSINESS OPPORTUNITIES

As long as the business world understands the issues arising from this great conflict of time – our lust for experience and varied lifestyles, the role of cultural activities in our identity/status and the continuing role of work within a set temporal space – then opportunities abound. The commercial world can help people not only to manage their time better and be happier as a result but to be successful too.

Despite our emphasis that convenience is not the only way to improve the satisfaction/time ratio it will remain a potent opportunity in many areas of life – specially with more mundane and tedious tasks. So, if satisfaction can be maintained (or even increased) while the time used is reduced then the innovation will be successful. Technology clearly has a big role to play here, hence our enthusiasm for developments like robotics that we discussed in Chapter 6. But there are great opportunities for service offers too (current examples are dry cleaning, take-away food, valet parking) and particularly those focused around home delivery since cutting travel time will be attractive.

But we believe the main scope is in increasing the satisfaction for any given unit of time. Not only does this mean always delivering superb products and services but also managing expectations as we noted earlier. But more than that it means understanding the needs, moods and expectations of the consumer. From that starting point new offers can be developed and existing ones improved to ensure that people are improving the time ratio of an activity.

Of course, implicit in all this is the belief that people will be prepared to spend more money for improved experiences (and better satisfaction/time ratios). This seems highly likely since we can expect affluence to continue to grow but time, on the whole, will not. But we wonder whether more of this increased spending will go on enhanced fulfilment rather than convenience. Certainly, to date people seem reluctant to pay very high premiums for convenience but are much happier (if they can afford it of course) to pay much more for highly regarded experiences. This is probably because the way time is valued is different depending on whether the activity is seen as enjoyable or a chore. On the whole we are used to paying for nice experiences but chores are often not something we pay for at all (apart from with our time). In the terms that economists might use, the price elasticity of time is lower for nice activities and higher for nastier ones, so we are more sensitive to price changes in the latter.

Of course, the ideal solution is to let consumers decide whether they want to focus on maximizing S or minimizing T – for as we said, the mood and personality of the consumer, and how this relates to a particular experience, is both highly variable and crucial to getting the equation right. Wherever possible, be this in call-centres, retail or leisure venues, consumers should be able to move through the experience at their own pace. Alternatively, businesses should be anticipating consumers' needs in relation to the S/T equation. Let us take the example of a weekday in the supermarket to illustrate this. In the morning, the majority of customers will tend to be older people, who are more likely to consider supermarket shopping more a pleasure than a chore, and whose time is unlikely to be under great pressure. After 5 p.m., though, the majority of customers will be doing 'top-up' shopping on the way home from work, and in an absolutely different frame of mind. How well can the environment adapt to the changing S/T equation of its customers? When do the express tills open? How many staff are on the shop floor, manning customer service, or behind tills at various times? Could the aisles themselves be reconfigured, rotated, re-stocked as the day goes by, creating a retail outlet that can shift from leisurely emporium to convenience store and back again? We don't think it is impossible.

On a broader level, one, as yet undeveloped, way that individuals can gain more time is by planning around the fact that we are living longer and healthier lives. Understanding this allows people to do a wider range of activities across their lives without overburdening themselves at any given point in time. In this instance people would deliberately plan to take up an activity at some later date when they had more time to do so. This already happens, of course, with the plans people make for retirement (to play golf, take up bridge or move to the south of France, for example) but we can foresee opportunities for doing this in a more structured way before that. There are opportunities in helping consumers prioritize activities across their life courses and in anticipating how such priorities might change over time (by perhaps monitoring life transitions – see Chapter 5).

There is one last, and rather fundamental, conclusion. Despite all this juggling of time and priorities, despite the potential to save time on chores by the use of technology or contracted labour; despite the potential to phase activities and experiences over a longer life-course, time is pretty finite. As more people have more discretion in how they use those time resources available to them and balance their different options (if not explicitly, then implicitly, in the way our formulae are set out earlier), so every activity is, in a sense, a competitor to every other. The competitive set that a company operates in is not some market or sector but the whole array of potential uses that someone can put that time to. Reminding consumers of this point (and perhaps attacking new 'competitors' in doing so) can be a potent marketing strategy.

CHAPTER 12

NAVIGATING A COMPLEX WORLD

*I*n March 2003, in a series of lectures at the London School of Economics, Professor Richard Layard – an eminent British economist – discussed the issue of happiness. He posed the question of why – despite being significantly richer than we were in the past – we are no happier. Note, there is no question that people are, on average, any less happy than they were in the past, as has been asserted by some commentators like Oliver James[1]. Indeed, as Layard pointed out:

> In the West we already have a society that is probably as happy as any there has ever been.[2]

No, the issue is that the massive gains in material wealth that have accrued to the western world in the last 50 years have not been translated into any significant increase in happiness. Why should this be?

THE HAPPINESS PROBLEM

Over the course of three evenings, Professor Layard put forward his views. He started by showing that happiness could be objectively measured and that the responses to survey questionnaires were comparable across the world. He went on to suggest that government policy should now, in the post-modern era, be focused on improving the well-being of all citizens rather than economic growth as such. He finished by arguing that income polarization, consumerism and a 'me first' attitude were to blame for the lack of improvement in happiness.

His point was that we are competitive souls and however much richer we get in real terms, it only leads to increased happiness if we are relatively better off than others. His proposed solutions were radical: more taxation not less; an encouragement for people to have more leisure; and limitations on advertising (he blames television for 'creating discontent' through exposing people to a vastly expanded range of comparisons).

There is clearly something in this – and particularly the point about leisure. The world is likely to be better for individuals and society as a whole if there is more leisure time and activities to fill it (it's no good having leisure but not the means or opportunity to use it, as often happens to the unemployed). There is even a persuasive economic argument why society should encourage leisure[3].

Equally, it seems obvious that relative affluence is important in happiness (as one of us has noted in the past[4]). But can the growing polarization of incomes in some countries really be the reason why happiness has not improved? After all, Britain has (and always has had) the same happiness rating as France but incomes have diverged more in the former than the latter in the last 20 years. The United States (one of the most income polarized countries in the western world, with a particular acceleration over the last two decades) has the same level of happiness as Denmark (one of the most income egalitarian states)[5].

Layard also notes an increase in anxiety and stress and links this to the failure to improve feelings of well-being. He wants more money spent on the treatment of mental illness – something that it would be hard to disagree with. But maybe this increase in reported stress provides a clue as to why happiness is not increasing. Is it that the sheer complexity of everyday life is making us feel more anxious? We think it is.

For the reasons we have outlined in this book – individualism, the waning influence of organizational structures and institutions, the growing importance of human capital (in all its forms) over material goods and financial capital, the greater life choices that health and longer lives afford us, the rapid roll-out of over-designed (or under thought through) technology, the cornucopia of consumer choices, less prescribed gender roles, more pressures on parenting, a growing range of fears and a desire for a fuller, more varied leisure portfolio – for all of these reasons, life is more challenging. And perhaps this is why despite our increasing wealth and freedom our happiness isn't growing. We are drowning the seeds of progress in the complexity of modern life.

Don't get us wrong. Not all complexity is bad. We have constantly pointed in this book to many of the positive aspects of modern life that have had the consequence of adding to life's choices. In many instances people welcome the freedom and variety that individualism, say, can bring. And, humans love to elaborate, investigate, and to be creative and innovative. This is what we might label *positive* complexity. On the other hand there are clearly instances of *negative* complexity. These would include excess choice for an individual consumer, unnecessary time pressures, information overload and an inability to judge risk and the anxieties that arise from that.

It is these *negative* complexities that are the main root of our woes and people need solutions to such problems. But people would welcome help with *positive* complexity too – tools that allow them to manage (and in some instance create) complexity – a fundamental component of a modern, rich life.

Business has a huge opportunity and a responsibility here. In this book we have outlined how business can help. We have concentrated on the consumer side but clearly there is also a lot to do in working patterns/conditions (what we ask and expect of people) and in supplier relationships.

Here, in summary, is what business could do.

PRODUCT AND SERVICE OFFERS

Our analysis identifies a number of areas where business could develop new products or services to help people manage the complexity of modern life. In no particular order these include the following areas.

Advisory services

There are clear opportunities for providing advice to consumers in a variety of instances. One of these is in helping people in product and service choices. This could either be recommendations on what to buy or help in how to make the right selection: what is the information that you need to know; what are the criteria you should be judging on? Many consumer magazines, newspaper supplements, Internet sites, TV and radio programmes already provide such services and we expect increased demand for them in the future.

In some instances, people might even be willing to delegate control of the selection process to experts – either individuals or well-known brands – asking such representatives to make the choice for them (and perhaps even to purchase the item as well). Retailers have a big potential role here if they can capitalize on consumers' trust. Already, the idea of retailers providing personal shoppers – who, for example, take note of an individual's needs and requirements to provide a reduced selection of clothes – is catching on. At another level there is the traditional retailer's function (as with butchers) of giving not only advice on what to buy but tips on how to use (cook) it. We expect to see more of this.

Such advice is not only about consumer products and services but also about life itself. Information or help on education and training options, job selection, even marriage guidance, could all see growing interest. Much of this is currently provided by public services but increasingly people are turning to the private sector too. The growth of counselling in its many forms is testament to the underlying need for these types of service.

Training, skills and networking tools

One specific area of service provision that we can see continuing to develop is that of training. We have made the point throughout the book that human capital is becoming increasingly valuable and therefore the need to build this up initially and then replenish and manage it will be critical. Not only will there be additional need for skills development at younger ages but adult education, and 'educational' content in the broadest sense, across all media, will be a big opportunity area too.

It is not just intellectual capital that people will seek to enhance but cultural capital as well. This suggests that there will be growth in demand not only for cultural experiences (see below) but also for the means to develop skills in these areas. Examples might be introduction courses to Japanese art or Cuban music, or specialist magazines or television programmes on food and wine or Italian renaissance art. Since, by its very nature, there are barriers to entry into certain cultural activities (in terms of not having sufficient skills or knowledge) there are good prospects in providing initial access to otherwise daunting areas: to provide entry level training.

We have also stressed how important social capital is in the network society. You cannot give people social capital as such but you can provide the tools or circumstances for achieving it. So, providing opportunities to meet and converse with others through gatherings, clubs, associations and virtual communities offers potential as does training programmes that help people develop their communication and networking capabilities.

These tools also include communications technologies in all their paraphernalia and guises. As we have pointed, out in a world where social capital is valued and social intercourse is welcomed it is not surprising that mobile phones, e-mail, instant and SMS text messaging have thrived. New software and platforms that add value to communication will continue to do so in the future.

Time management

For all the reasons we outlined in Chapter 11, people will carry on valuing help in time management. So, technology products – both hardware and software – that assist in this will continue to do well. This will fuel growth in communication and other devices that allow consumers more flexibility in what they do and where they do it – and hence greater ability to manage their time. There are critical questions here that all businesses should ask themselves. Are you giving people greater control over what they can do and when? Are you helping to solve people's time problems? If not, then at the very least make sure you do not leave them with inconvenient delivery times or products that do not work immediately and efficiently. Less severe, but still dangerous, is inflicting frustrating 'dead time' on customers, through queuing, delays, or inefficient customer response mechanisms. Even where a time-cost is inevitable, there is no excuse for *wasting* it. Some supermarkets in the United States have televisions above the tills so shoppers can catch up with the latest news while queuing.

British Airways' flat beds on its long-haul flights can be seen as a mechanism for helping people manage their time – having slept better they can make more efficient use of time the following day.

As we have made clear this does not just mean providing convenience solutions, although there will be opportunities for that. It also involves people being able to create 'spaces' in their busy lives: time oases as we have put it. So there will be good opportunities for activities that seem to slow the pace of life or allow people to relax and let it all go just for a while. The success of health spas can be seen in this context and they and other similar pursuits – the long weekend at a rural idyll or the week on the beach in the sun – will continue to be popular. The opportunity is to discover new offers that tap into this potential.

There is a branding corollary here (as we noted in Chapter 1) – are you a slow brand associated with reflection and time 'space' or a fast brand associated with problem-solving and time-saving?

Convenience

People will also look for things that save them time so the convenience concept has lots of mileage in it yet. This particularly applies to those areas creating unsatisfying time pressures (like household chores) or activities where time could be saved (like picking up shopping or a hire car). British car rental firm easyCar is testing the pick-up of hire cars from everyday places – streets or shopping malls for instance – using mobile communications devices to 'unlock' the car for the approved customer. The time benefits over having to go to a central location to collect the hire car are likely to be attractive to many consumers and although the result is much the same as having the car delivered to your home, it is a lower cost option for easyCar.

Other opportunities exist for 'time-doubling' – allowing people to overlap two activities. We provided in an earlier chapter the example of getting your dry cleaning done while you are at the cinema but there are a range of other possibilities like having your car cleaned while at the supermarket. You get the idea.

We have also pointed to the way technology can help to save time, particularly in the home. There has been, and always will be, a great consumer interest in technology products that relieve the chores of washing, cleaning and other less desirable household tasks. But technology can help too in more pleasurable activities – making the cooking of food easier while delivering better quality (think here of bread and ice cream makers), or allowing television programmes to be recorded and watched at one's convenience.

Design for use

The example of time-shifting focuses attention on a crucial issue for technology: user-centred design. The video recorder, as we have noted, is a classic example of how not to design a product. Of course what it does at a fundamental level (time-shift) is hugely helpful, which explains its success. But the way it has been implemented – seemingly deliberately to confuse and increase the chance of mis-recording – is horrendous. The message is clear: design for ease of use and with the user in mind; do not presume the more features the better; there may well be a growth in 'simplified' technologies that have basic, but predictable functionality.

Flexible products

In the area of financial services, and perhaps other service providers, there is the potential to provide more flexible products that can cope with and adapt to the changes of circumstance that occur throughout people's lives. Targeting products at specific groups (say, single professionals or a couple with young children) risks losing those customers when they move into a new life-stage. Better, surely, to provide a product that can adjust to people's lives rather than the other way round. Flexible mortgages (and the success of them) illustrate the potential here.

But this can be extended to family or wider groups. Why not more flexible banking for couples which combines a joint account with independent ones too? This merely reflects the reality of what is already happening with people having a joint account for bill payments but retaining individual accounts for personal use. But why should these be spread across different retail banks rather than being in just one?

Equally, young people could benefit from the credit rating of their parents or the funds that their grandparents have accumulated but do not, at present, need. Such arrangements already occur on an informal basis (interest-free loans to grandchildren, parents buying car insurance under their name for their children) but why not offer family accounts or family insurance, thus locking in the whole family to the financial service provider (and easing financial headaches too).

The importance of experience

All service providers need to recognize the potential of placing more 'experience' into their offers. This will include an extension of what is already happening in some retail outlets where shopping is simply made more fun. As Pine and Gilmore put it:

> Think about a pure retailer that already borders on the experiential. The next time you go to a Sharper Image or a Brookstone – two retailers that provide a place where consumers can play with the latest high-tech devices – watch the customers as they meander around the store . . . Could such an establishment charge admission? . . . The retailer might very well sell more goods.[6]

This is more than time-doubling as we just described it (where in this instance people could do their chore shopping and have an enjoyable leisure experience) since it can also include re-categorizing an activity from chore to pleasure. In this sense, the more 'culture' (and we certainly do not only mean high culture here) and ludic elements that can be put into the offer the better.

But the trends we have discussed and especially those concerning cultural capital and individualism suggest that the desire for leisure experiences in a variety of forms will continue to grow.

CUSTOMIZATION

Individualism means people often want individual solutions. This is not always true – where the product or service is of no interest, commoditized or is completely functional, consumers may be happy with mass-market solutions. Big, solid, trusted brands come to the fore here (see below). But in many sectors we envisage that the market will develop in different ways to meet the fragmentation of customer needs. Some people, particularly at the higher end of the market, will look to hand-made, authentic products providing unparalleled uniqueness. The alternative will be mass customization that will provide an element of difference but at a price people can afford. Mass customization can take the form of built to order but it could equally be more and more differentiation of brands and sub-brands so long as these can be provided in an economic way (there are clearly distribution and marketing costs to consider). The course of action will depend on the product and market in question.

Business commentator Alan Mitchell has taken this further – and into the realm of services too – with his concept of 'solution assembly'. This places the consumer at the heart of the business with the role of the company being to solve that customer's problems:

> Look at any important aspect of 'my life' – my finances, my health, home maintenance, home replenishment, my transport/logistics – and what companies bring to market the ingredients of the solutions I need? Invariably, there is something else I have to do to get the

outcome I really want – something that requires additional work, time, energy, expertise, expense etc.; something that costs me more than the price of the product or service itself.

Solution assemblers go beyond the dictates of traditional vendor efficient supply to focus on customer efficient demand instead. They help me address these additional integration and coordination costs to reduce them and/or improve the final result.[7]

COMPETITIVE SET

As we want to do more and more and at a rate that exceeds the time available (even allowing for work-time reductions and extra time from longer lives) so time does become a more precious commodity. In this sense, as we discussed in the last chapter, every activity, every market, is in competition with every other. All businesses are doing one of two things: competing for people's time; or providing people with more time. In this way, the money spent on a microwave oven could also be spent on a dishwasher or even a faster transport option for commuting. All are trying to save people time. (We accept that these are not the only reasons why people buy microwave ovens or make their transport choices.) Equally, any activity that will use, rather than save, time is competing for those precious minutes. It could be a restaurant, a football match, a new hi-fi system. Companies must not solely focus their attention on their own market and own competitors but should take a broader view of the consumer's life and needs.

BRANDING

Choice managers

We have discussed at length the ways in which consumers tackle the often overwhelming array of choice they face. Brands, as editors, as choice managers, have a key role to play. For this very reason, Naomi Klein is wrong – we are not facing a future without brands and without logos[8]. What is critical here are brands that have a clear proposition (for example Sony stands for innovative, quality electronics) and are trusted (which is likely to be generated by its overall stance to business – see citizen brands below – and the reliability and consistency of its delivery). From this base, brands can develop sub-brands that provide the necessary navigation tools in a complex market while catering for individual choice too.

Citizen brands

As we say, one way of building trust – and a bank of goodwill towards an organization – is to become a citizen brand: a brand that recognizes that it has a role in, and set of relationships with, society as a whole[9]. A 'good' company (ethical, good employer, environmentally aware) is not only specifically chosen by some enthusiasts but is generally given more leeway and more time to respond to actual or perceived mistakes. In a world of increasing volatility and anxieties, fluctuations in market shares and attitudes to products and brands are likely to be greater. Being a citizen brand can help to 'smooth' this as it has more credibility when addressing scares or 'scandals'.

Related to this are the opportunities to build upon the growing interest in communities and belonging that arise from the seemingly more uncertain world. One element of this is localism, another is communities of interest. If a company has local or regional associations, it should flaunt them. If it can tap into a special interest group or life event, as in our example of the *Huggies Club*, it should do so. Allowing people to relate their own life stories and attachments to an organization consolidates the sense that the organization understands its role in the wider community.

In the same vein, there are possibilities to build on the heritage or authentic roots of a brand where they are relevant to the modern world or the community at large.

The three layers of branding

Another aspect of branding is its role in differentiation and identity. But there is a potential conflict here with the softer aspects of 'belonging' that we have just described. This desire for individualism and the need for inclusion are not as contradictory as it seems. But this does present problems for brands. Which is it: a differentiator or a coagulator? Overarching corporate brands and more individualized sub-brands may be the answer.

But all brands have to consider where they are on three levels:

- Basic functional delivery – what does the product or service do and how well does it do it? Although achieving certain levels on this is now a baseline requirement, brands can still differentiate themselves in this way.
- Inclusive values (citizen brand) – how does this company operate and do I want to be associated with it? This is becoming an increasingly important aspect of consumer decision-making.
- Differentiation – how does this brand differentiate me from (or associate me with) others?

The relative importance of these will vary for different markets and different segments of the population. But we would make two points. First, consumers are increasingly cynical about brands and are therefore likely to use them in a much more functional, yet capricious way. Second, young people are much more positive about brands, needing them for choice management and identity purposes. With an ageing population, the focus of marketing and branding will need to accept this, as we noted in Chapter 5.

Managing brands in the network society

In a network society, where people not only have more contacts but rely on them more for advice and support (as a result of reduced deference to institutions), personal recommendations, and recriminations, have more weight. Understanding the dynamics of word-of-mouth and considering how it might be managed will be critical. The idea of managing such a mercurial process seems daunting but we would provide the following simple advice:

- Increase positive word-of-mouth by: giving people a reason to say good things about a brand; understanding who are the critical people in the network (the 'mavens' and 'connectors' as Malcolm Gladwell describes them in his book *The Tipping Point*[10]); and maximizing the 'stickyness' of the message[11].
- Decrease negative word-of-mouth by: delivering consistently good service (so there is no reason for criticism); and generating trust and involvement (so people will discount any negative messages and forgive the occasional mistake).

SEGMENTATION

For a whole range of reasons segmentation is just going to get harder. For a start, age stereotypes are becoming decreasingly useful as age is less of a constraint to both attitudes and behaviour. Forget gender caricatures too. And individualism and the fragmentation of markets will just make segmentation more and more complex. If you are going to use a traditional segmentation then life-stage is probably the best for the moment but even that will become less efficacious. Two strategies should be considered, however.

Mode

Segmentation methods need to recognize that people's needs, attitudes and behaviour are dependent on the circumstances and specifics of a given occasion. As we have pointed out, people have multifarious 'modes', so an individual can be one 'type' of person in one instance (with a certain set of needs) and a rather different one in another. This is one of the most important outcomes of a complicated society.

Segmentation techniques therefore sometimes need to be based on the occasion rather than the person as such.

Transitions

But within these multiple layers of individuality it remains the case that certain life events do have a reasonably predictable effect. Having children changes people's priorities, outlook on life, roles within the household, time pressures, responsibilities and leisure pursuits (amongst other things). Buying a house (or just moving property) and leaving work (enforced or chosen) can prompt equally dramatic changes to needs and demands. Understanding these life 'triggers' is potentially a fruitful alternative to traditional segmentation techniques. If you can quantify such effects (which is possible by analysis of longitudinal datasets like the British Household Panel Study[12]) and identify them, then marketing activity can be planned accordingly. As a mechanism, this is about tapping into life's realities and requires a re-engineering of the company to respond to the consumer's contemporary needs. In this way it is another form of the solution assembly discussed earlier.

FINAL THOUGHTS

We hope we have shown that consumers' lives are indeed more complicated. Understanding this plain fact, and its complex ramifications, presents wonderful opportunities for business. But we cannot claim that this is easy – indeed, tackling life's complications, and helping consumers manage them, just makes things more complex for business too. In that sense, the one simple conclusion from our research is that there are no simple answers anymore.

We have shown that progress, in itself, creates complexity. There is little one can do about this because, for individual citizens, the positive aspects of advancement outweigh its negative effects. So solutions will be needed to life's complications and if a company does not help consumers in this way, they will find one that will – this is not a business decision that can be shirked. Not least because, not only is it a good business opportunity but it is a chance to add to the sum of human happiness. Who could resist that?

NOTES

INTRODUCTION

1. For example, Stewart Lansley, *After the Gold Rush: The Trouble with Affluence: 'Consumer Capitalism' and the Way Forward*, London: Century, 1994. A more recent example is Professor Richard Layard's 2003 Lionel Robbins Memorial Lectures at the London School of Economics on the subject of 'happiness' (http://cep.lse.ac.uk/events/lectures/).

2. An example of someone who is concerned about the technological determinism that is behind the development of technology just because it is possible without any regard for human need or sensitivity is Langdon Winner, professor of political science in the Department of Science and Technology Studies at Rensselaer Polytechnic Institute in Troy, New York. As Winner notes: 'Again and again, we are urged to celebrate the latest so-called "innovations" regardless of the deranged commitments and disastrous consequences they often involve.' (Source: http://www.rpi.edu/~winner). His books on this theme include *The Whale and the Reactor: A Search for Limits in an Age of High Technology*, University of Chicago Press, 1988.

3. See, for example, Lee Burns, *Busy Bodies: Why Our Time-obsessed Society Keeps Us Running in Place*, New York, W.W. Norton, 1993.

4. Or even, the effective demise of work – see Jeremy Rifkin and Robert L. Heilbroner, *The End of Work: The Decline of the Global Labour Force and the Dawn of the Post-Market Era*, New York: Warner 1995.

5. Juliet Schor, *The Overworked American*, New York: Basic Books, 1991.

6. Robert Putnam, *Bowling Alone: The Collapse and Revival of American Community*, New York: Simon and Schuster, 2000.

7. Richard Sennett, *The Corrosion of Character: The Personal Consequences of Work in the New Capitalism*, New York: W.W. Norton, 1998.

8. Neil Postman, *Amusing Ourselves to Death: Public Discourse in the Age of Show Business*, New York: Viking, 1986.

9. Richard Layard, op. cit. See also, the World Database of Happiness at www.eur.nl/fsw/research/happiness/index.

10. We might personally exclude some military technologies from this analysis.

11. In this sense, this book complements one that we have previously produced – Michael Willmott, *Citizen Brands*, Chichester: John Wiley & Sons, 2001.

CHAPTER 1: IT'S A COMPLICATED LIFE

1. The number of books bought by the average household continues to increase although the time spent reading is falling.

2. For example, Abraham Maslow, *Motivation and Personality*, New York: Harper, 1954 and Ronald Inglehart, *Modernization and Postmodernization*, Princeton University Press, 1997.

3. The so-called 'prosumer', where the consumer communicates directly (even to the factory) their own specifications, is suggested as far back as 1985 by Alvin Toffler in *Future Shock*, London: Pan Books, 1985.

4. Manuel Castells, *The Rise of the Network Society*, Oxford: Blackwell Publishers, 1996.

5. Jeremy Rifkin, *Age of Access: How the Shift from Ownership to Access is Transforming Modern Life*, London: Penguin, 2000.

6. Marshall McLuhan, *The Medium is the Massage: An Inventory of Effects,* with Quentin Fiore, New York: Bantam, 1967; London: Allen Lane, 1967.

7. When one of us was interviewed on a nationwide British radio show, the presenter just could not understand why having too much choice was a problem. (Although he did admit that he never went to the grocery store himself as his wife did all the shopping!)

8. One of us tends to turn to Sony first thanks to its reputation for innovation and the quality of its products. It might not be the final

choice but as a filtering process it narrows the field and makes decision making simpler.

9. Peter Willmott, *Family and Class in a London Suburb*, London: Routledge and Kegan Paul, 1960; Robert and Helen Lynd, *Middletown: A Study in Modern American Culture*, Harvest Books, 1959.

10. Phyllis Willmott, *Bethnal Green Journal: 1954–1955*, London: Institute of Community Studies/Future Foundation, 2000.

11. Frank Furedi, *Paranoid Parenting*, London: Allen Lane, 2001.

CHAPTER 2: THE NEW INDIVIDUALISM

1. Or more precisely, *reflexive* – see Ulrich Beck, Anthony Giddens and Scott Lash, *Reflexive Modernisation: Politics, Tradition and Aesthetics in the Modern Social Order*, Cambridge: Polity Press, 1994.

2. Office for National Statistics, *Social Trends 2002*, London: Stationery Office, 2002.

3. J.K. Galbraith, *The Affluent Society*, Boston: Houghton Mifflin, 1958.

4. Watts Wacker, Jim Taylor and Howard Means, *The Visionary's Handbook: Nine Paradoxes that will Shape the Future of Your Business*, New York: HarperBusiness, 2000.

5. Abraham Maslow, *Motivation and Personality*, op. cit.

6. See, for example, Ronald Inglehart, *Modernization and Postmodernization*, op. cit.

7. Naomi Klein, *No Logo*, London: Flamingo, 2000.

8. *New Statesman*, November 2002.

9. Michael Willmott, *Citizen Brands*, op. cit.

10. nVision is a subscription service from the Future Foundation that combines an extensive online data and analytic resource with workshops and briefings about future trends. It includes a consumer research programme, Changing Lives, that conducts surveys on a regular six-monthly basis. Trends can be tracked back to the early 1980s.

11. A term first used by Watts Wacker, Jim Taylor and Howard Means in their book *The 500 Year Delta*, New York: HarperBusiness, 1997.

12. 'Purchased' either directly, through private education, or indirectly, through 'opportunity hoarding' in geographical areas or social networks that exclude the less wealthy. See Pierre Bourdieu, *Distinction: A Social Critique of the Judgement of Taste*, London: Routledge, 1984.

13. nVision (see earlier footnote) has a European service. Consumer research conducted for the service in 2002 shows that the proportion agreeing that 'the brand of clothing I wear is important to me' ranged from four out of ten in Italy to just over one in four in Britain to one in six in Spain and Norway.

14. Mintel, *Retail intelligence*, 2001 (authors' own analysis).

15. BBC News Online, 23 January 2002, http://news.bbc.co.uk/1/hi/ sci/tech/1775496.stm. See also, www.vertu.com.

16. Susan Greenfield, *The Private Life of the Brain*, London: Penguin, 2002.

17. Ibid.

CHAPTER 3: THE ROUTELESS SOCIETY

1. Francis Fukuyama, *The Great Disruption: Human Nature and the Reconstitution of Social Order*, New York: Simon and Schuster, 2000. For a provocative – yet we believe valid – critique of this book see: http://www.modelreasoning.com/.

2. www.weforum.org.

3. Gordon Gekko – the main character in Oliver Stone's 1992 film *Wall Street* and played by Michael Douglas – pronounced that 'greed is good'.

4. Robert Putnam, *Bowling Alone: The Collapse and Revival of American Community*, op. cit.

5. Harris Interactive, August 2002.

6. Harris Interactive, November 2003.

7. *Business Week*, Special Report – *Scandals in corporate America*, 8 July 2002.

8. Michael Willmott, *Citizen Brands*, op. cit.

9. Mike Hall, *How Advertisers Think Marketing Works*, British Market Research Society Annual Conference, 1991 and *How advertising works: new steps on the advertising timeline*, Paper given to the APG Conference – Boston, 1998. For a summary of Hall's thesis and the other models he proposes, see also Michael Willmott, *Citizen Brands*, op. cit.

10. *The Responsible Organisation*, London: BT/Future Foundation, 1997 (available from the Future Foundation).

11. Robert Putnam, *Bowling Alone*, op. cit.

12. Richard Florida, *The Rise of the Creative Class*, New York: Basic Books, 2003.

13. Dora Costa and Matthew Kahn, *Understanding the Decline in Social Capital 1952–1998*, Cambridge: National Bureau of Economic Research, 2001 and others quoted in Richard Florida, *The Rise of the Creative Class*, op. cit.

14. Richard Florida, *The Rise of the Creative Class*, op. cit.

15. Roger Mitton and Michael Willmott, *A social forecast revisited*, forthcoming. This paper discusses the change in leisure pursuits by comparing research on leisure participation conducted in 2001 with similar research from 1971 and published (together with forecasts for the year 2001) in P. Willmott and M. Young, *The Symmetrical Family*, London: Routledge and Kegan Paul, 1973.

16. Peter Willmott, *The Enduring Extended Family*, forthcoming.

17. *Changing Britain, Changing Lives: Three Generations at the Turn of the Century*, Edited by Elsa Ferri, John Bynner and Michael Wadsworth, Institute of Education, University of London, 2003.

18. Ibid.

19. Richard Florida, *The Rise of the Creative Class*, op. cit.

20. Charles Leadbeater, *Up the Down Escalator: Why the Global Pessimists are Wrong*, New York: Viking, 2002.

21. Peter Drucker, quoted in *Wired Magazine*, March 1998.

22. Jonathan Gershuny, *A new measure of social position: social mobility and human capital in Britain*, Institute for Social and Economic Research, 2002; John Ermisch and Marco Francesconi, *Intergenerational social mobility and assortative mating in Britain*, Institute for Social and Economic Research, 2002.

CHAPTER 4: HUMAN CAPITAL AND THE NETWORK SOCIETY

1. Economists originally developed the term 'human capital' in the 1960s and 1970s to refer specifically to the skills and capabilities that can be applied in the labour market. But it is now sometimes used in sociological circles to mean the three components identified here – or 'embodied capital' as Bourdieu described it. There is, thus, some confusion when people talk about human capital but we use it here (for all its faults) in the broader sense and not just to mean labour market skills and capabilities.

2. Pierre Bourdieu, *Distinction*, London: Routledge, 1984.

3. Jonathan Gershuny, *Time, through the Lifecourse, in the Family*, Institute for Social and Economic Research, 2003.

4. Sorokin, as summarized by Gershuny, *A new measure of social position: social mobility and human capital in Britain*, op. cit.

5. Richard Berthoud and Jonathan Gershuny (Editors), *Seven Years in the Lives of British Families*, Bristol: The Policy Press, 2000.

6. The most often quoted example of this is the ethos at American retailer Nordstrom where employees are lectured on the importance of customers and that they should do whatever is needed to keep them satisfied – quoted in various places including James Collins and Jerry Porras, *Built to Last*, London: Century Books, 1996.

7. Some might argue that mentioning the creative and consulting industries together like this is an oxymoron.

8. Charles Leadbeater, *Living on Thin Air*, New York: Viking, 1999.

9. Richard Florida, *The Rise of the Creative Class*, op. cit.

10. Ibid.

11. Jeremy Rifkin, *Age of Access*, op. cit.

12. Ibid.

13. Jonathan Gershuny and Kimberly Fisher, *Leisure in the UK Across the 20th Century*, Institute for Social and Economic Research, Essex University, 1999.

14. Stephen Hawking's acclaimed *A Brief History of Time* (London: Bantam Books, 1988) has been translated into 33 languages and sold over 9 million copies but we have met many people who admit to owning the book but never, in fact, having read it.

15. Jeremy Rifkin, *Age of Access*, op. cit.

16. John Ermisch and Marco Francesconi, *Intergenerational social mobility and assortative mating in Britain*, op. cit.

17. Jonathan Gershuny, *A new measure of social position: social mobility and human capital in Britain*, op. cit.

18. Personal conversation with Jonathan Gershuny.

CHAPTER 5: NEW LIFE COURSES, NEW CHALLENGES

1. In some countries, they still do. Italian men, for example, are not only delaying marriage but also lead their European neighbours in the age

they leave home, to the extent that they have been labelled 'Mummy's Boys' by the Rome based Psychology Institute of the National Research Council. In some other countries like Britain, young men (and women) do still leave home at an historically early age but are increasingly likely to return at some point, as we show in Chapter 9.

2. Ulrich Beck, Anthony Giddens and Scott Lash, *Reflexive Modernisation: Politics, Tradition and Aesthetics in the Modern Social Order*, Cambridge: Polity Press, 1994.

3. Peter Willmott and Michael Young, *The Symmetrical Family*, op. cit.

4. A recent example is Jonathan Gershuny's analysis of time-use by life-stage, *Time, through the Lifecourse, in the Family*, op. cit.

5. Manuel Castells, *The Rise of the Network Society*, op. cit.

6. nVision, Changing Lives survey, op. cit.

7. The term 'vertical family' was first described by sociologists Peter Willmott and Michael Young.

8. *Shopping Centre Futures*, 2002 – available from British Council of Shopping Centres and Future Foundation

9. Analysis by Willmott and Nelson on behalf of Mothercare (unpublished). See also: Jonathan Gershuny, *Time, through the Lifecourse, in the Family*, op. cit.

CHAPTER 6: TECHNOLOGY AND COMPLEXITY

1. Richard Florida, *The Rise of the Creative Class*, op. cit.

2. nVision/Future Foundation.

3. Harris Interactive, April 2002.

4. nVision Europe/Future Foundation.

5. nVision, Changing Lives survey/Future Foundation.

6. James Gleick, *Faster: The Acceleration of Just About Everything*, London: Abacus, 2000.

7. Postman has written for years on this subject and indeed recognizes that he is seen as 'anti-technology' and a 'dinosaur' (he stills write with pen and paper) but he has some valid takes on the use and rollout of technology, as we note later. See his recent book, *Building a Bridge to the 18th Century*, Vintage Books, 1999.

8. John Kenneth Galbraith, *The New Industrial State*, New York: The New American Library, 1968, p. 19.

9. Langdon Winner, *Autonomous Technology: Technics out of Control in Political Thought*, Cambridge, MA: MIT Press, 1977.

10. James Gleick, *Faster: The Acceleration of Just About Everything*, op. cit., p. 174.

11. *Complicated Lives Report*, published as part of our research programme for British bank Abbey National and available from the Future Foundation.

12. *Interface: User and Machine*, RSA, London, 6 November 2002.

13. *Complicated Lives Report*, Abbey National/Future Foundation, op. cit.

14. Manuel Castells, *The Rise of the Network Society*, op. cit.

15. *Do modern communications technologies make life better or worse*, BT Social Policy Team/Future Foundation. Available at http://www.btplc.com/Betterworld/PDF/Qualityoflife.pdf.

16. Ibid.

17. Michael Willmott, *Citizen Brands*, op. cit.

18. *M-Commerce*, a research study conducted by the Future Foundation, 2001.

19. Watts Wacker, Jim Taylor and Howard Means, *The Visionary's Handbook*, op. cit.

20. Neil Postman, *Building a Bridge to the 18th Century*, op. cit.

CHAPTER 7: THE CHOICE EXPLOSION

1. Adam Smith, *An Enquiry Into the Nature and Causes of the Wealth of Nations*, London: Penguin, 1982. In the same section Smith says of shopkeepers and tradesmen that: 'So far is it from being necessary, either to tax them, or to restrict their numbers, that they can never be multiplied so as to hurt the publick, though they may so as to hurt one another.'

2. Jean Paul Sartre, *Existentialism and Humanism*, London: Methuen, 1987.

3. Family Expenditure Survey, National Statistics/nVision/Future Foundation.

4. *The Appearance of the Millennial Woman*, Pretty Polly/Future Foundation, 2001.

5. *The Future of Bill Payment*, nPower/Future Foundation, 2000.

6. We were advised by UK telecoms regulator Oftel (now called Ofcom) to consider three as the absolute minimum number of fixed-line suppliers that the average UK consumer could choose from.

7. These figures are estimated from the brochures of the mobile phone retailer Car Phone Warehouse.

8. Ofgem, *Experience of competition in domestic electricity and gas markets*, 2001.

9. *The Future of News*, Ananova/Future Foundation, 2001.

10. We wondered how we might factor in news on the Internet to our calculations. A search for 'news' on Google produced no less than 119 million hits. We realized that quantifying news on the Internet was difficult not only because of the ocean of information out there, but also because of the unclassifiable nature of most of this information – what would we classify as 'nationally available news' in this environment?

11. Jon Elster, *Solomonic Judgements: Studies in the Limitations of Rationality*, Cambridge University Press, 1988.

12. We should perhaps think of 'regulators' in the broadest sense: increasingly, NGOs, the media, scientists, all make direct attempts to influence or circumscribe markets.

13. James Gleick, *Faster: The Acceleration of Just About Everything*, op. cit.

14. Ofgem, *Experience of competition in domestic electricity and gas markets*, op. cit.

15. nVision/Future Foundation.

16. Ibid.

CHAPTER 8: REGENDERING LIFE

1. *New York Observer*, 21 October 2002.

2. See Helen Wilkinson, Melanie Howard and Sarah Gregory, *Tomorrow's Women*, London: Demos, 1997.

3. Despite the recent release of data showing that full-time women's hourly wage as a proportion of men's fell back slightly in 2002 – this is explained by an increase in top income earners' salaries, most of whom are men, rather than a falling away for the female workforce. Excluding the top 20% of earners, women's wages rose 4.6% in 2002, compared with 4.1% among men. However, accelerating incomes at the top of the range are an important proviso here – 'fat cat' wages will continue to be appropriated by men for the foreseeable future.

4. National Management Salary Survey/nVision.

5. *Complicated Lives Report*, Abbey National/Future Foundation, op. cit.

6. British Household Panel Study (authors' own analysis, in conjunction with Dr Jonathon Scales, ISER).

7. Indeed, 'traditional' notions of adults' gender roles have been thoroughly bound up with *parental* roles – and, as we discuss in Chapter 5 the amount of adults' lives spent as a parent has declined by around a half.

8. *Complicated Lives Report*, Abbey National/Future Foundation, op. cit.

9. Anyone who has had to 'negotiate' domestic labour with a partner will not be surprised that there is a consistent (around 10%) discrepancy between the reports of men and women.

10. Jasmine Burnley, Mark Hepworth and Anne Green, *Women and the Knowledge Economy*, University of Warwick, November 2001. Available at http://www.btinterface.co.uk/reports/report_pdfs/Women_Knowledge_Economy.pdf.

11. Quote from Future Foundation qualitative research for Abbey National, 2001.

12. *Complicated Lives II*, Abbey National/Future Foundation, op. cit.

13. Ibid.

14. Anecdotal evidence suggests that the 'balance of control' can be highly market specific. In any case, the overall trends suggested by our data indicate an erosion of this bifurcation of control. Increasingly, service providers or companies wanting to sell products on hire purchase will find it less profitable to target one gender or another, and more likely to find their offer subject to a process of negotiation between both partners.

15. Data from 1991 to 1995 collected in the British Household Panel Study, Institute for Social and Economic Research. Data from 2002 collected by Future Foundation/Marks & Spencer.

16. Gershuny and Lawrie's analysis in *Seven Years in the Lives of British Families*, op. cit. suggests that a woman's likelihood of having an equal say in financial decisions is most strongly associated with whether or not she is in employment.

17. *Complicated Lives Report*, Abbey National/Future Foundation, op. cit.

18. Mass Observation Archive, University of Sussex. Note that it was focused on working-class women.

19. Quote from Future Foundation qualitative research for Abbey National, 2001.

CHAPTER 9: THE PARENTING CHALLENGE

1. Frank Furedi, *Paranoid Parenting*, op. cit.
2. Jonathan Gershuny, first published in *Prospect* magazine, but similar patterns are observable in Jonathan Gershuny and Kimberly Fisher, *Leisure in the UK Across the 20th Century*, op. cit.
3. John Robinson and Geoffrey Godbey, *Time for Life*, University Park, PA: Penn State University Press, 1997.
4. Jonathan Gershuny and Kimberly Fisher, *Leisure in the UK Across the 20th Century*, op. cit.
5. *Complicated Lives Reports*, Abbey National/Future Foundation, op. cit.
6. Even when taking into account the effect of inflation, four out of five parents (80%) think that they spend more on their children's birthday presents than their own parents spent on them at that age. Only 12% think they spend the same, and 8% think they spend less. *Complicated Lives Reports*, Abbey National/Future Foundation, op. cit.
7. *Complicated Lives Reports*, Abbey National/Future Foundation, op. cit.
8. Mass Observation Archive, University of Sussex, Brighton, England.
9. This woman was aged 60 at the time of the Mass Observation survey so was presumably talking about a period around 1900. Mass Observation Archive, op. cit.
10. *Complicated Lives Reports*, Abbey National/Future Foundation, op. cit. One in ten claimed that pressure from the children (pester power) was the most important aspect, while one in six openly accepted that it was so their children could keep up with others. Other responses included that they had gone without when the parents were them-selves children and they did not want their children to experience the same, and that it was a reward – that the children deserved it. Both of these were selected by around one in ten of respondents.
11. *Complicated Lives Reports*, Abbey National/Future Foundation, op. cit.
12. David Gordon *et al.*, *Poverty and Social Exclusion in Britain*, London: Joseph Rowntree Foundation, 2000. See also the work of Professor Peter Townsend.
13. P. Willmott and M. Young, *The Symmetrical Family*, op. cit.
14. Authors' analysis of Britain's Office for National Statistics, 2000 Time Use survey.
15. *Complicated Lives Reports*, Abbey National/Future Foundation, op. cit.
16. Special analysis by the Future Foundation of the British Household Panel Study 1996–2000, run by the Institute for Social and Economic

Research, Essex University and funded by the Economic and Social Research Council.

17. Frank Furedi, *Paranoid Parenting*, op. cit.

18. In a survey 58% of parents agreed that they worried about 'being over-protective', as compared with just 22% who worry about 'giving children too much freedom'. *Public Agenda,* New York, reported in *The Wall Street Journal*, 13 March 2003.

19. *Complicated Lives Reports*, Abbey National/Future Foundation, op. cit.

20. Ibid.

21. Mass Observation Archive, op. cit.

22. Ibid.

23. *Complicated Lives Reports*, Abbey National/Future Foundation, op. cit.

24. Quoted in 'Ageing: bopping until we drop; ripe old age is becoming a more pleasing prospect than in Shakespeare's day', Nicholas Timmins, *Financial Times*, 5 February 2000.

25. *Complicated Lives Reports*, Abbey National/Future Foundation, op. cit.

26. Frank Furedi, *Paranoid Parenting*, op. cit.

27. Extract from the UN convention taken from Michael and Terri Quinn, *From Pram to Primary School,* Family Caring Trust, 2002. (A good example of a successful modern 'guide-book' for parents.)

28. *Complicated Lives Reports*, Abbey National/Future Foundation, op. cit.

29. Authors' analysis of British Household Panel Study, 1996–2000, op. cit. See also Chapter 5.

30. *Complicated Lives Report*, Abbey National/Future Foundation, op. cit.

CHAPTER 10: THE ANXIETY SOCIETY

1. Aaron Wildavsky, quoted in Slovic, 'Perceptions of risk', *Science*, 1987.

2. Frank Furedi, *The Culture of Fear* [updated], Continuum, 2002.

3. Barry Glassner, *The Culture of Fear*, New York: Basic Books, 1999.

4. 'BSE fears eat into McDonalds profits', *The Guardian*, 25 January 2001.

5. 'Food risks seen and denied, in brief', *International Herald Tribune*, Italy Daily, 15 January 2001, quoted in Spiked Online: http://www.spiked-online.com/Articles/00000000547A.htm.

6. 'Probe gives Buffalo Grill a rough ride', *Financial Times*, 7 January 2003.

7. Michael Willmott, *Citizen Brands*, op. cit.

8. Barry Glassner, *The Culture of Fear*, op. cit.

9. Bjorn Lomborg, *The Skeptical Environmentalist*, Cambridge University Press, 2001.

10. All European and North American countries share in this trend – we show only selected countries for the sake of clarity.

11. Human Mortality Database. University of California, Berkeley (USA), and Max Planck Institute for Demographic Research (Germany). Available at www.mortality.org or www.humanmortality.de.

12. 'Does the Internet make us lonely?', *European Sociological Review*, 2000; 16: 427–438.

13. Jonathan Gershuny, *Web-Use and Net-Nerds: A Neo-Functionalist Analysis of the Impact of Information Technology in the Home*, Institute for Social and Economic Research, Essex University, 2002.

14. Ulrich Beck, 'Living your life in a runaway world', in *On the Edge*, edited by Anthony Giddens and Will Hutton, London: Jonathan Cape, 2000.

15. Christopher Wanjek, *Bad Medicine: Misconceptions and Misuses Revealed*, Chichester: John Wiley & Sons, 2003.

16. 'When journalists juggle figures, the public is at risk', *The Age*, 7 August 2002, http://www.theage.com.au/articles/2002/08/06/1028157932945.html.

17. Melvin A. Benarde, *You've Been Had!: How the Media and Environmentalists Turned America into a Nation of Hypochondriacs*, Rutgers University Press, 2002.

18. Steven Bratman, *Health Food Junkies: Overcoming the Obsession with Healthy Eating*, New York: Broadway Books, 2000.

19. 'Praise the lard', *The Observer*, 11 August 2002.

20. Melvin A. Benarde, *You've Been Had!*, op. cit.

21. Bjorn Lomborg, *The Skeptical Environmentalist*, op. cit.

22. Michael Fitzpatrick, *British Medical Journal*, August 2002.

23. Michael Willmott, *Citizen Brands*, op. cit.

CHAPTER 11: COMPLICATED TIMES

1. Pierre Bourdieu, *Outline of a Theory of Practice*, Cambridge University Press, 1997, referencing Gary Becker, 'A theory of the allocation of time', *Economic Journal*, 75, no. 289, September 1965.

2. For an interesting discussion see Leon Kreitzman, *The 24 Hour Society*, London: Profile Books, 1999.

3. Michael Young, *The Metronomic Society*, London: Thames & Hudson, 1988. See also the writings of Lewis Mumford.

4. Leon Kreitzman, *The 24 Hour Society*, op. cit.

5. John Robinson and Geoffrey Godbey, *Time for Life*, op. cit. or Jonathan Gershuny, *Changing Times*, Oxford University Press, 2000.

6. Richard Florida, *The Rise of the Creative Class*, op. cit. quoting updated figures from John Robinson and Geoffrey Godbey, *Time for Life*, op. cit.

7. Jonathan Gershuny, *Changing Times*, op. cit.

8. Ibid.

9. Oriel Sullivan and Jonathan Gershuny, *Cross National Changes in Time-Use: some Sociological (Hi)stories Re-examined*, Institute for Social and Economic Research, Essex University, Working Paper 2001–01, 2001. This paper provides a useful overview of time-use trends in industrialized countries, looking specifically at trends in paid work, unpaid work, leisure and personal care and discussing why there is a discrepancy between popular concepts like 'time famine' and the 'reality' of time-use diaries.

10. John Robinson and Geoffrey Godbey, *Time for Life*, op. cit.

11. Interviews conducted as part of our research programme for British bank Abbey National and published in the *Complicated Lives* series of reports (available from the Future Foundation).

12. Ibid.

13. Canada, Denmark, Finland, Netherlands, United Kingdom and United States.

14. Jonathan Gershuny, *Time, through the Lifecourse, in the Family*, op. cit.

15. Richard Florida, *The Rise of the Creative Class*, op. cit. quoting the work of Robinson and Godbey.

16. Jonathan Gershuny and Kimberley Fisher, *Leisure in the UK Across the 20th Century*, op. cit.

17. Oriel Sullivan and Jonathan Gershuny, *Cross National Changes in Time-Use: some Sociological (Hi)stories Re-examined*, op. cit.

18. Peter Willmott and Michael Young, *The Symmetrical Family*, op. cit.

19. James Gleick, *Faster: The Acceleration of Just About Everything*, op. cit.

20. John P. Robinson and Geoffrey Godbey, *Time for Life*, op. cit.

21. Lee Burns, *Busy Bodies: why our time-obsessed society keeps us running in place*, op. cit.

22. Richard Layard, Lionel Robbins Memorial Lectures, op. cit.

23. Richard Tomkins, 'How to be happy', *Financial Times*, 7 March 2003.

CHAPTER 12: NAVIGATING A COMPLEX WORLD

1. Oliver James, *Britain on the Couch: Why are we Unhappier Compared to the 1950s – Despite Being Richer?*, London: Arrow, 1998.
2. Richard Layard, Lionel Robbins Memorial Lectures, op. cit.
3. Jonathan Gershuny, *Changing Times*, op. cit.
4. Michael Willmott, *Citizen Brands*, op. cit.
5. World Database of Happiness, directed by Ruut Veenhoven, Erasmus University Rotterdam, http://www.eur.nl/fsw/research/happiness/index.htm.
6. B. Joseph Pine and James H. Gilmore, *The Experience Economy – Work is Theatre and Every Business a Stage*, Harvard Business School Press, 1999.
7. Alan Mitchell, Gerhard Hausruckinger and Andreas Bauer, *The New Bottom Line: Bridging the Value Gaps that are Undermining your Business*, Capstone Wiley, 2003.
8. Naomi Klein, *No Logo*, op. cit.
9. Michael Willmott, *Citizen Brands*, op. cit.
10. Malcolm Gladwell, *The Tipping Point*, Boston: Little, Brown and Company, 2000.
11. Ibid.
12. The British Household Panel Study is managed by the Institute for Social and Economic Research at Essex University and funded by Britain's Economic and Social Research Council.

INDEX